Teen Devotionals... for Girls! volume 2

Written by Shelley Hitz, Heather Hart
and Contributing Authors

Brought to You By:

Teen Devotionals...For Girls! Volume 2

Copyright © 2012 by Shelley Hitz, Heather Hart and contributing authors

All rights reserved. No part of this publication may be reproduced, stored in a retrieval system, or transmitted by any means – electronic, mechanical, photographic (photocopying), recording, or otherwise – without prior permission in writing from the author, unless it is for the furtherance of the Gospel of salvation and given away free of charge.

Body and Soul Publishing

ISBN-13: 978-0615631622
ISBN-10: 0615631622

Printed in the United States of America
All scripture quotations, unless otherwise indicated, are taken from the Holy Bible, New International Version® 1973, 1978, 1984 by International Bible Society. Used by permission of Zondervan Publishing House. All rights reserved.

Learn more information at:

www.FindYourTrueBeauty.com
www.ShelleyHitz.com

Presented to:

From:

Date:

This book is dedicated to our
Lord and Savior, Jesus Christ.

For from Him and through Him and for Him are all things. To Him be the glory forever! Amen.
~Romans 11:36

Contents

INTRODUCTION 1
1. TRUE BEAUTY 2
2. WILLFUL SIN 4
3. HAIR 6
4. SOMEBODY 8
5. DEPRESSION 10
6. DATING 13
7. LOVABLE 16
8. TRUST 18
9. ONE-SIDED 21
10. RESCUED 23
11. EYE-CATCHING 26
12. EXCLUDED 28
13. CONVERSATIONS 31
14. PEOPLE VS. THINGS 34
15. POSSIBILITIES 36
16. WITHERING BEAUTY 38
17. FRIENDSHIPS 41
18. FORGIVENESS 43
19. ONE OF A KIND 45
20. BEHAVIOR 47
21. ANCHORED 49
22. CASTING STONES 52
23. ANXIETY 55

24. ALL POWERFUL 58
25. UNPLEASANT CIRCUMSTANCES 60
26. GOD'S GLORY 62
27. EQUAL 65
28. PEER PRESSURE 67
29. CHALLENGE 70
30. SECURITY TAG 72
31. HUNGER 76
32. WAKE UP! 79
33. BIG ENOUGH 83
34. INTIMIDATION 85
35. EMPTY 87
36. CHECKLIST 90
37. REMEMBRANCE 93
38. WEARY 95
39. ASK 97
40. KNOCKED DOWN 99
41. CHASING DREAMS 101
42. DEVOTED 103
43. JOB 105
44. QUIET TIME 107
45. PERFECT 110
46. FORGETFUL 112
47. OBEY 114
48. SPIRITUAL CLOTHING 118
49. IN HIS NAME 120

50. MARY'S SONG	123
51. WHY?	126
52. SCARS	130
53. COMMISSIONED	133
54. A LESSON FROM HAITI	135
55. SELF-IMAGE	139
56. ATTITUDE	142
57. HOPE	144
58. BLACK AND WHITE	146
59. PASSIONS	149
60. THE PRICE	152
61. PRAYER & PRAISE	155
62. ANGER	157
63. SURRENDER	160
64. ENSLAVED	162
65. PMS	165
66. KINDNESS	167
67. OUR SAVIOR'S STANDING	169
68. SHARING	172
69. LONELY	174
70. CHILDLIKE FAITH	177
71. FILLING THE VOID	180
72. A FICKLE FOLLOWER	183
73. PROMOTING LOVE	185
74. THE SABBATH	187
75. ON GOALS & MOTIVATION	189

76. BAD HAIR DAY 192
77. THE NEW KID 195
78. GENTLENESS 198
79. PRAYING TOGETHER 200
80. BE YOURSELF 202
81. LEFTOVERS 205
82. THRIVE 207
83. LIGHTING THE WAY 210
84. WITNESSING 212
85. NOT SHAKEN 215
86. WHEN I FAIL… 218
87. LIFE'S LEMONADE 221
88. AGEISM 224
89. PURITY 228
90. JESUS-CHUTE 231
CONCLUSION 235
RECOMMENDED RESOURCES 236

Introduction

This is the second book of *Teen devotions... For Girls!* brought to you by FindYourTrueBeauty.com. Our desire is to help you draw closer to God by finding your true beauty in Christ. We hope that as you read through these devotionals you will grow in your walk with God, and that you will be able to relate God's Word to your life in a relevant way.

Because these devotions are designed specifically with teen girls in mind, you can read through them anyway that works for you. You can flip through and read just the ones that you want, or read from front to back. You can read one each morning, before bed, or even just one per week. You can read them by yourself, with a friend, or in a group. There are no guidelines. We understand that every Christian walk is different and we just hope that these devotions can be of some help to you along the way. If you have questions, comments, or just need someone to talk to, please feel free to contact us using the contact information at the end of this book.

"Now I commit you to God and to the word of his grace, which can build you up and give you an inheritance among all those who are sanctified."
~Acts 20:32

True Beauty

Is it what I wear?

Written by Heather Hart

...Which is greater: the gold, or the temple that makes the gold sacred?

~Matthew 23:17

Have you ever stopped to think about where your beauty comes from? While we have heard that our true beauty comes from Christ, we still put a huge emphasis on our outer beauty. We take the time to put on makeup, do our hair, and pick out the clothes that we think will make us look the best. Sometimes we even think that without those things, we are nothing. We find our value in the things that we put on our bodies, instead of in Christ. The Word of God tells us that our bodies are God's temple (1 Cor. 16:9), and Jesus took the time to remind us that it isn't the gold (or the makeup or clothing) that makes the temple great.

Our beauty doesn't come from the things we put on, but from the Holy Spirit living inside of us. True beauty can't be stolen, it doesn't wash off, and it doesn't fade over time. True beauty is everlasting, never failing, and it grows as time goes by. It isn't what we put on that makes us beautiful, but the evidence of our growing relationship with Jesus Christ that radiates from us. That is what truly makes us great!

Reflection:

Do you think your true beauty comes from what you wear, or from the inside?

Application step:

When you get ready for the day, remember that it isn't what you put on that makes you beautiful. When you get ready for bed take a moment to praise God that your true beauty can't be taken off or washed away.

Prayer:

Father God, please help me to remember that my beauty doesn't come from clothing, makeup or jewelry, but from you. You made me beautiful, a temple for the Holy Spirit. It isn't what I wear that makes me who I am, but you living inside me. Help me to remember that, and help my true beauty to grow as I draw closer to you. In the name of your Son, Jesus Christ, I pray. Amen.

Willful Sin

What choices do you make?
Written by Heather Hart

Keep your servant also from willful sins; may they not rule over me. Then will I be blameless, innocent of great transgression.
~Psalm 19:13

Have you ever made a decision to do something that you knew was wrong? Maybe your mom or dad asked you a question and you told them something that wasn't quite the truth, or even an all out lie. Maybe you cheated on your homework or a test. Perhaps you talked bad about someone behind their back, and maybe even said something that wasn't true. There are so many ways that we choose to sin every day. We choose to let our circumstances dictate us and our behavior, rather than what we know to be the right thing. We often are so caught up in the here and now that we don't think about the eternal consequences. We know that lying is a sin, we know that cheating is bad, and we know that it is wrong to gossip. These are just a few examples of the ways that we choose to sin each day. Your struggle with sin might be more physical. You could be choosing a sin of mistreating your body by starving yourself, overeating, cutting, masturbation, or engaging in premarital sex. While none of us our perfect, God has promised us that if we turn to Him, He will help us. We can pray for Him to help us overcome the habitual sins in our life that are there because we are allowing them to be. He can give us the strength to live a life that is pleasing to Him, and a life that we can be proud of.

Reflection:

What are the willful sins in your life?

Application Step:

Pick a sin that you habitually choose to commit even though you know that it is wrong, and make a commitment to stop. Pray for God to help you, and when temptation arises make the choice to stand firm in your resolve. Try looking up some verses about your particular sin, and writing them in a notebook or on a note card and carrying them with you.

Prayer:

Father God, I know that I have sin in my life that is only there because I choose for it to be. I make decisions in the moment, and don't always think things all the way through. Help me to make the right choices, help me to choose to do what will please you, and what I know is right. Help me to turn to you in the hour of my temptation, and help me prevail over sin. In the name of your son, Jesus Christ, I pray. Amen.

Hair

Placed with care
Written by Heather Hart

And even the very hairs of your head are all numbered.
~Matthew 10:30

God values us so much that He has numbered every hair on our head. In some cultures women are required to cover their heads because men find the women's hair so attractive. Think about it for a minute, how much time do you spend each day brushing, washing, or fixing your hair in some way? Quite a bit, right? Why do we do that? Our hair is one of the first things other people notice about us. Could you imagine going out today without combing your hair...

God loves us so much that He gave us our hair, and He didn't just throw it up there and let it grow, He placed each strand with care. Could you imagine how long it would take to count them all? I can't, but God already has. He gave us our hair to cover our heads, and make us beautiful. Some of us wear our hair down, and others pull it up or style it in some way. We all know that our hair is part of who God made us, and we need to remember that God made us beautiful. So whether you have long hair, short hair or no hair, remember that God knows. He doesn't long for you to have the shade of hair that your best friend's mom has, or curls like your brother's girlfriend does. He doesn't yearn for you to have more hair, less hair, thicker or thinner hair. He made you just the way He wanted you, and

He placed each strand of hair with loving care. God put variety in the world for a reason. How boring would it be if we all had hair like your Auntie Em?

Reflection:

Do you recognize your hair as a gift from God? Have you ever taken the time to thank Him for it?

Application step:

When you spend time fixing your hair today, take a moment and thank God for it. Thank Him for giving you your hair, for making it perfect, just the way He wanted.

Prayer:

Father God, in the past I haven't appreciated the hair you gave me as I should. I have dyed it, highlighted it, curled and straightened it, trying to make it more beautiful. I have neglected the fact that you placed each strand with care, please forgive me for that. Help me to see your love for me when I look in the mirror, and whenever I take the time to care for the hair that you have given me. In the name of Your Son, Jesus Christ, I pray. Amen.

Somebody

Are you a 'nobody' or a 'somebody'?
Written by Heather Hart

For God so loved the world that he gave his one and only Son, that whoever believes in him shall not perish but have eternal life.

~John 3:16

There's an old song sung by Dean Martin that says "You're nobody 'till somebody loves you". If I had to hazard a guess, most of us would agree with that statement in one way or another. We often find our worth in what others think or feel about us. We try to impress others with our knowledge, our clothing, trying to please them with our actions. The truth however, is that we are loved more than we could ever imagine and not by just someone, but by the creator of the universe! If we need to find our worth in what someone else thinks about us, we should look to Him. He loves us so much that He sent His Son to die on the cross for our sins! He loves us so much that He rejoices when we turn to Him, and He loves us so much that delights in us. There is nothing that could ever separate us from the love of Christ (Romans 8:38-39), He loves us that much!

So if we are nobody until somebody loves us, we should be rejoicing in the love of Christ. We should see ourselves as somebody in Christ. God obviously sees us as somebody's. In fact, He see's us as enough of a 'somebody' to send His Son to die for us. That is something to put value in. We aren't nobody's, we are children of God, redeemed through the death and resurrection of His Son, Jesus Christ, and we know that we will not perish but have everlasting life! Hallelujah!

Reflection:

Where do you look to find your worth? Do you know that you are a 'somebody' through Christ?

Application Step:

Take some time and reflect on what God has done for you, and who you are in Him.

Prayer:

Father God, you are so glorious! Thank you so much for sending your son, Jesus Christ, to die for my sins so that I could be forgiven and live eternally with you! Help me to remember that I am a somebody, and that you love me more than I could ever ask or imagine. You are so wonderful Lord! In the name of your Son I pray. Amen.

Depression

Sing out loud!
Written by Heather Hart

Why are you downcast, O my soul? Why so disturbed within me? Put your hope in God, for I will yet praise him, my Savior and my God.

~Psalm 43:5

Why are you downcast, O my soul? A more modern way to word that question would be: Why am I so depressed?! I don't know about you, but I get depressed sometimes. I mean, let's face it life is hard. Not only is it hard, but it can be downright depressing! It seems like there is always something that isn't going the way that I think it should. Someone says something about me that isn't very nice (or maybe downright mean), I'm not allowed to do something with my friends that I really wanted to, or maybe I wasn't even invited, or maybe the guy that I liked just started dating my best friend. Maybe it's something bigger like you have to move, or you're parents are getting divorced… The list of possibilities is endless, but you want to know something? One thing I have noticed is that I am only depressed when I'm focused on me. If I am busy praising God, I forget that I am depressed. Let me tell you, it is so hard to be depressed while singing worship songs!

There are lots of different ways to cope with depression, but I have truly found that the best way is to remember that God loves me. The things of this world, while they are the here and now, won't last. I use to get so mad when my mom would say something like, "it's just high school, it only lasts for 4 years". It made me want to scream. I mean, anyone who has ever been to high school should know that it is the LONGEST 4 years of your life, and for those 4 years it IS your life. I'm not trying to make it sound like it isn't a big deal, but I have come to realize that the individual events that happen each day, usually are forgotten in a week or two. So I wasn't allowed to go to the mall with my friends, there's always next time, and even if I'm not allowed to go next time, I will still see them tomorrow. As for that guy dating my best friend, either I need to be happy that she is happy, or realize that I really didn't need him in my life, and I am better off without him. God knows everything that I need in my life, and He will provide everything that I need in His timing, not mine.

Reflection:

Do you frequently find yourself depressed? How do you handle your depression?

Application Step:

Next time you're feeling depressed, turn on some praise and worship music. Sing at the top of your lungs about how awesome our God is!

Prayer:

Father God, I am so thankful for you! You know all of my needs, and you always take care of me. There are times when all I can see is the here and now, and I get depressed Lord. It's so hard to look forward when life seems to be weighing me down. Help me to remember that you are awesome, no matter what life throws my way. Help me to praise you through the storms, and get through life's depressing moments by focusing on you. In the name of your Son, who you sent to die on the cross for me, I pray. Amen.

Dating

Is he good for you?
Written by Heather Hart

Do not be yoked together with unbelievers. For what do righteousness and wickedness have in common? Or what fellowship can light have with darkness?
~2 Corinthians 6:14

I'm pretty sure that we have all heard this verse quoted at some point in time or another, but have you ever stopped to think about why God would give us this instruction? God doesn't just go around making rules at random, or forbidding fun things just for spite. He always has a purpose, and He always has our best interests at heart.

It took me a while to learn that God told us not to date unbelievers not because they weren't great people, or good friends, but because when we commit ourselves to dating someone, we do so to get closer to them. God knows that if we commit to drawing closer to an unbeliever, it will ultimately draw us away from Him. However, if we date another Christian, then while we are learning more about them, and drawing closer to them, we will also be learning more about God and drawing closer to Him. The best example I have ever heard about this was when a friend of mine related it to a triangle. Triangles have 3 points, 3 angles and 3 sides. If you were to put God at one point, you at another, and then your boyfriend or crush at the third, what kind of a triangle would you have? Would you be closer to God or your boyfriend? If your boyfriend is not drawing closer to God and has no desire to do so, then you can either move closer to your boyfriend or closer to God, but you have to make the choice. BUT if you are equally yoked together with another Christian, then you have an equilateral triangle and as you and your boyfriend draw closer to God, you will move closer together as well.

If you choose to date that unbeliever, are you going to choose to go hang out with him on Sunday morning or go to church? Are you going to ask him to pray with you before you eat dinner at a restaurant? What about if you go on to get married, are you going to be able to read the Bible to your children, take them to church, and celebrate holidays in a way that honors Christ, or will you have to submit to living a life void of Christ?

Reflection:

Is your relationship drawing you closer to Christ, or pulling you away?

Application Step:

Take sometime today and pray about your relationship (or desired relationship). Ask God if it is pleasing to Him, or if there are changes that you need to make. Then ask Him to give you the wisdom and strength to make those changes!

Prayer:

Father God, I'm so glad that you don't make rules just so there are rules. I must admit that I don't always understand why some things aren't allowed, but I trust that you have my best interest at heart. Lord, I need your help in my relationship. I want to date someone that will help me grow in my relationship with you, not draw me away. Please give me the strength I need to make the right decisions in the coming days. In the name of your son, Jesus Christ, I pray. Amen.

Lovable

Can God love a sinner like me?
Written by Heather Hart

On hearing this, Jesus said to them, "It is not the healthy who need a doctor, but the sick. I have not come to call the righteous, but sinners."

~Mark 2:17

Satan loves to tell us lies, and loves to spin stories that make us believe things that aren't true. One of the lies that he likes to lead us to believe is that God could never love us because of our sin. We know that God is a loving God, but we don't believe that He could ever possibly love us... Does this sound familiar? Have you ever thought that way? When Jesus was on earth He took the time to tell us that He didn't come to call the righteous, but the sinners. You see, we are all sinners. The Bible also tells us that there is not a soul on earth that does what is right and does not sin (Romans 3:10) and if we claim to be without sin we make God out to be a liar (1 John 1:10). We are all sinners. I'm a sinner, you're a sinner, and even your pastor is a sinner. The way Jesus put it is that if we weren't sinners and we never sinned, then He wouldn't have needed to come to die for us. But the reality is that we are sinners, and He loves us so much that He did come to die on the Cross so that we could be saved from our sins. Jesus is the only person who ever lived that never sinned, and that's why it's by His blood that we are saved. And the best part is that there is no sin to great to be forgiven, there is no sin big enough that the blood of Jesus can't cover it.

Romans 8:5 puts it this way: *"But God demonstrates his own love for us in this: While we were still sinners, Christ died for us."* God loves us even though we sin. He knew we were sinners, yet He loved us so much that He sent His one and only begotten son to die for us, so that we could go to heaven to be with Him for all eternity. There is nothing that can ever separate us from the love of Christ (Romans 8:38-39).

Reflection:

Do you believe that God loves you even though He knows what you did yesterday, last week and last year?

Application Step:

Take sometime today to sit down and confess your sins to God, and then thank Him for loving you despite your sins.

Prayer:

Father God, it never ceases to amaze me that you who are so perfect and holy could love a sinner like me. Please forgive me for my sins, and help me to live a life that brings glory to you. Help me to overcome the sin in my life, Lord. And please help me to remember that you love me, even when I screw up. In Jesus name I pray. Amen.

Trust

Trusting in Time

Written by Heather Hart

But grow in the grace and knowledge of our Lord and Savior Jesus Christ.

~2 Peter 3:18a

There are many people that I trust in life. However, I didn't trust any of them the first day that I met them. In order for me to learn to trust them, I had to first learn more about them. I'm sure that you understand that, and probably come to trust people the same way. It just takes time to learn to trust someone. The more we spend time with them and get to know them, the more we trust them or know just how untrustworthy they are. The same principle applies to our walk with God. The first time that we were told about God, we didn't instantly trust Him with our lives. It took hearing more about Him, and then eventually we gave Him our hearts, but our journey wasn't over there.

We have to keep spending time with God and keep learning more about Him in order for our trust to grow and develop. Let's think about it this way. Do you remember your best friend from kindergarten? Is that person still your best friend today? Do you still trust them? If you needed them to come over right now and let you cry on their shoulder, would they? Or would you say that you have drifted apart over the years? Maybe it was abrupt because one of you moved. You tried to keep in touch, but in the end it just wasn't the same. Maybe you both still live in the same town but you have just drifted apart. You stopped spending time together or became part of different clicks. Now what about your current best friend? Did you become best friends and instantly trust each other the first time you met, or do you trust them more now than you did the first day you saw them? The same thing happens with our relationship with God. He is just as trustworthy today as He was 10,000 years ago, but we didn't know Him back then. He will always be trustworthy, even 200 years from now, but if we don't spend time with Him, our trust in Him will drift. We will forget how trustworthy He is, and start to be bogged down by the troubles of life. On the other hand, the more time we spend with Him, and the more we get to know Him through His word and prayer, the more we will learn to trust Him, and see what a wonderful friend He is.

Reflection:

Do you trust God? Do you spend time talking with Him and learning more about Him each day?

Application Step:

Spend some one on one time with God today. Read His word, and just sit and talk with Him for a while.

Prayer:

Father God, thank you for being who you are. It's so wonderful to know that I can trust you with anything and everything! Please help me to continue to grow closer to you, Lord. Help me to want to spend time with you, help me to enjoy reading your Word. Lord, help me to trust you more. In the name of your precious son I pray, Amen.

One-Sided

What kind of a friend are you?
Written by Heather Hart

A man of many companions may come to ruin, but there is a friend who sticks closer than a brother.
~Proverbs 18:24

Have you ever been in a one-sided friendship? You know, where you consider someone a friend and always take the time to listen to them and help them out, but they never do the same for you? One of those friendships where you would be there no matter what when they need you for anything, but you probably can't count on them to be there for you? Have you ever had a friend who didn't really care how you were doing? If you have you know that it doesn't feel good.

Have you ever been one of those friends? Have you ever been the friend that is never there for the other person? Most of us don't like to think of it that way, but to be honest, most of us have probably failed to be a good friend at some point in time during our lives. Most of us try to be good friends to others, but what about in our relationship with God? He's always there for us, but how much do we take that for granted? I know God never needs us, but how often do we go a week without speaking to Him? How often do we just kind of forget about Him until we need something?

If you're anything like me, the answer to those questions is probably more often than you should. While God is always ready and waiting for us, we often put Him on a back burner because we know He isn't going anywhere. We focus on other friendships that aren't as sure of a thing, taking the most important relationship we have and belittling it.

Reflection:

Is your relationship with God one-sided?

Application Step:

Make an effort today to do something for God, not yourself. It could be anything from helping or encouraging someone, to donating something to someone in need. Then, give God the credit and remember to thank Him for using you for His glory.

Prayer:

Father God, you are so wonderful, but I have to admit that I often take you for granted. You are the friend that sticks closer than a brother, and I am a girl with many companions that often forgets you are there. I tend to only remember you when I am feeling down or need help with something. Please forgive me for that. I don't want my friendship with you to be a one-sided friendship. I want us to have a strong friendship. Please help me to be a better friend to you, and not to take advantage of your amazing love for me. In the name of your son, Jesus Christ, I pray. Amen.

Rescued

Prince charming to the rescue!
Written by Heather Hart

He lifted me out of the slimy pit, out of the mud and mire; he set my feet on a rock and gave me a firm place to stand.
~Psalm 40:2

Most girls have dreamed of being rescued by their prince charming at some point in their lives. We dream of him riding up on a big white horse, and carrying us away. We grow up watching movies of princesses trapped in castles or lying in a deep sleep, just waiting for their prince charming to come to the rescue.

Do you want to know something though? Our prince has already come. He came 2000 years ago to rescue us. His work was completed when He laid down his life for us. Death could not hold our prince though, because our prince is the prince of peace. He is the only perfect human that ever lived and much more, He isn't just some fairy tale. No, our prince is real and death couldn't keep Him in the grave because death is the penalty for sin, and our prince is sinless. Our prince rose from the grave after 3 days and is now sitting by His Father's side in heaven, waiting for the day when He is allowed to return to bring us home with Him. He already saved us. He lifted us up out of the slimy pit, out of the mud of sin, and He set our feet on solid rock and gave us a firm place to stand. He told us that since He had saved us, He was going to go and prepare a place for us. Our princes saving work is completed, we are saved through Him, and Him alone. How wonderful it is to know that He didn't just abandon us after saving us, but that He went to make a new home for us, where we will be able to spend all eternity safe from harm.

So next time you are feeling down, and long for a prince to come to carry you away, remember that you have a prince, and He is coming back soon to bring you home. Wouldn't it be a good idea to be ready?

Reflection:

Are you thankful that Christ our prince of peace came to rescue us from sin? Are you ready and eagerly awaiting His return?

Application Step:

Remember to thank God for sending Jesus to rescue us from sin. Show God that you are thankful by praying for Jesus' return, and ask God to help you be ready to greet Him with a smile!

Prayer:

Father God, I am so thankful that princes don't just exist in fairy tales, but that you truly did send a prince to rescue me. Thank you so much! I would be lost in a sinking world if it weren't for what Jesus did for me. I know that someday Jesus is going to come back to bring me home, and I pray that until that time comes that I will remember all that He has done, and is doing for me. Help me to honor my prince with my life, so that when He returns I can greet Him with my arms wide open. In the name of my prince, the Lord Jesus Christ, I pray. Amen.

Eye-Catching

Clothing vs. Character
Written by Heather Hart

Your beauty should not come from outward adornment, such as braided hair and the wearing of gold jewelry and fine clothes. Instead, it should be that of your inner self, the unfading beauty of a gentle and quiet spirit, which is of great worth in God's sight.

~1 Peter 3:3-4

What do you think the first thing people notice about you is? Do you think the first thing they notice is your hair, your clothing, or your figure? Do you put out an extra effort each day to make sure that you look great? Today's verse tells us that our beauty shouldn't come from our outward adornment, but from our inner self. So what about your character? Do you think that people notice how you treat and respond to others? Do you think that people can tell that you are a Christian by the way you act and the words you say? Do you put in that extra effort each day to spend time with God in hopes of becoming more like Him?

Sometimes I forget that the clothes that I put on in the morning, I take back off at night, but the time I spend building a relationship with God, lasts for eternity. 20 years from now no one is going to remember the way that I did my hair today, but they will remember how I treated them. They will remember if I professed to be a Christian, but my actions didn't back it up. But they probably won't have a clue what my shoes looked like or what color of eye shadow I wore to the prom. When I look at life from that perspective, I no longer desire to catch someone's eye with my clothing, but I want them to notice my relationship with Christ through the way I interact with others.

Reflection:

Do you want others to notice you for your looks or for who you really are?

Application Step:

Make a commitment to spend more time on your relationship with Christ than on your outward appearance.

Prayer:

Father God, I love you. I really do. However, sometimes I fail to show that. I tend to get caught up in the things of this world. I want to look good for others Lord, but I can't seem to remember that it's not my hair or clothing that really makes an impact on others. The condition of my heart and how that effects my actions is what leaves a lasting impression on those that I meet. Lord, I don't want to be remembered as a hypocrite. I want to be remembered as someone who brought glory to your name. Please help me to become the person you want me to be, and to put less of my focus on things that really aren't that important in the long run. In the name of your precious son, Jesus Christ, I pray. Amen.

Excluded

Do you ever feel left out?
Written by Heather Hart

Blessed are you when men hate you, when they exclude you and insult you and reject your name as evil, because of the Son of Man.

~Luke 6:22

Have your friends ever left you out of something, just because they know you are a Christian? Or have your parents ever told you that you couldn't do something, because it went against the Christian beliefs? It doesn't make you feel very blessed to be a Christian does it? However, I think that this takes on a whole new meaning when you look at it from God's point of view. Let's say that one of your friends decided not to go to a party, just because you weren't going. How would you feel then? You would probably be grateful that you had such a good friend. What if one of your friends stood up for you, even when you weren't around? That would be pretty cool too. What if because they stood up for you, they weren't invited to a party, or were un-invited to the mall? You would be totally psyched that they cared that much about you, wouldn't you. But what if they decided to go without you, ignored others who were mocking you, or even joined in? You wouldn't feel very loved would you? My guess is that your feelings would be hurt, and you would start to wonder if they were really even your friends. God is the same way; He doesn't just want us to love Him when it's convenient for us, but always. He wants us to stand by Him even if that means that we miss out on something, just as we would want our friends to do for us. God isn't saying that we are blessed because we are hated, but rather that we are blessed because we know what's most important in life. It isn't some party, or trip to the mall, but a personal relationship with Christ that causes true blessings to flow.

Reflection:

Which do you think is more important, going to a party, or standing up for your faith in Christ?

Application Step:

The next time that you get left out of something just because you are a Christian, remember how you would feel if it was one of your friends choosing to miss out on something because they loved you.

Prayer:

Father God, there are times when it doesn't feel like much fun to be a Christian. Everyone else goes off and does things that I know aren't right, and I feel left out, Lord. I don't really want to do the things that they are doing, but it still hurts to be excluded and insulted. Help me to remain strong during these times, Lord. Help me to remember that true friends stand by one another, even if it means they get left out. Help me to remember, Lord, that if the shoe was on the other foot, I wouldn't want one of my friends going somewhere that I wasn't invited, or hanging out with people who made fun of me and doing nothing about it. Remind me of those thoughts when I need to remember them, and give me the strength to stand up for you. In the name of your Son, Jesus Christ, I ask these things. Amen.

Conversations

Who could your words hurt?
Written by Heather Hart

Besides, they get into the habit of being idle and going about from house to house. And not only do they become idlers, but also gossips and busybodies, saying things they ought not to.
~1 Timothy 5:13

"Can you believe that she is in there playing that song again? She plays it every day!"
"More like 100 times a day, it is so annoying!"
"Yeah, and when she's not playing it, she's playing that other one that's even worse!"
"Oh I know! I can't stand that one"

Have you ever had a conversation like that? It happens to be one that I overheard at church this past weekend. While these two teen girls were thinking they were speaking privately, I heard them. If I heard them, someone else probably did too. What if the girl they had been speaking about had heard them? How do you think she would have felt? Or what if I would have been her mom, or even their mom?

A lot of people wouldn't even consider that gossip, but the definition of gossip is to talk casually or maliciously about other people, I'm pretty sure that it fits the bill. The Bible is extremely clear on its stance against gossip. Romans 1:29 lists it among its list of wickedness and evil. Ephesians 4:29 tells us that our words should be used to build others up, that our words should be beneficial to those that listen. I don't think that anything beneficial came out of that conversation, in fact, it could have caused a lot of pain considering the girl they were speaking of was considered a friend of theirs. But don't we all have conversations like that? I know that I am guilty of having them. It's just much easier to see them when it's someone else doing the talking.

Reflection:

Would I have every conversation that I have, even if the person that I was talking about was there? Do I think about the feelings of others before I speak?

Application Step:

Before you get involved in a conversation, ask yourself if it is a conversation building others up, or gossiping about someone who isn't there. If you can, find an accountability partner! Join together with a friend who can make this commitment with you so you can help each other along the way.

Prayer:

Father God, it is so easy to talk about other people. When things bother me, or when I notice things, it seems like such a natural response to tell someone. Please help me to remember that some things are better left un-said and others should only be said to the person they are about. Gossiping only serves as temporary entertainment for me, and can ultimately hurt others. Please Lord, help me to think before I speak. Help me to remember that other people have feelings and even if I never intend for them to hear my words, they might. In the name of Jesus I ask these things, Amen.

People vs. Things

What do you value most?
Written by Heather Hart

Give to everyone who asks you, and if anyone takes what belongs to you, do not demand it back.
~Luke 6:30

Have you ever had someone take something that belongs to you; maybe something as simple as your sister "borrowing" your favorite shirt without asking, or someone at school taking something out of your lunch? If so, Jesus' words here in Luke probably weren't high on your list of favorite things to hear at the time. Does Jesus really want us to not stand up for ourselves? Does He really expect us to stand by and let others take our stuff, and then what little we have left just give it away? Maybe, but I don't think that was really His point when He spoke those words. I think His main point was really that we should love others as we love ourselves (Matthew 22:39). We should put the value of people above the value of material items. The desert from your lunch tray is quickly eaten, your favorite shirt will eventually wear out and need thrown away, but the way that you treat other people, will be remembered long after. Your sister probably won't even remember stealing your clothes in a few years, but she will remember if you loved her more than the things in your closet. That kid at school won't remember what flavor the yogurt was, but he will remember that you showed Him kindness.

The point is that while the things of this world are here now, they don't last and they usually aren't even remembered. However, when we let Christ love others through us, the impact we can have on them can be eternal. Which is more important to you: your favorite shirt, or your sister's salvation?

Reflection:

Do you put more value into material items that are temporary, or in the eternal state of others souls?

Application Step:

The next time that someone takes something that belongs to you, let them. Instead of throwing a huge fit, tell them that they are more important to you than material things, and if it is really important to them that they can keep it.

Prayer:

Father God, there are so many times that I put the value of the things of this world above that of your children. Please forgive me for this, and help me to remember what you value most. Thank you for loving me, Lord. Help me to love others the way that you would, and to remember that people are always more important than things. Amen.

Possibilities

It seems impossible...
Written by Ashley McCollough

Jesus looked at them and said, "With man this is impossible, but with God all things are possible."
~Matthew 19:26

Many of us today try to look into the future at what we might want to do in life, and sometimes those dreams can seem impossible. Some of us long to be a singer, writer, or even a professional athlete; all of these things (and anything else that you can dream of) are in reach to anyone, even us. God puts desires deep inside of us, and if the desire is from Him there is nothing that can keep us from fulfilling our dreams!

If God is calling you to do something that seems impossible to achieve, always remember "with God all things are possible." As long as you have God on your side you can do anything through Him. It's not impossible, it may seem unthinkable to even image, but you have to trust Him and know that nothing will be impossible for you when you have God on your side.

Reflection:

Does what God is calling me to do seem impossible?

Application Step:

Take your first step in this journey that God is setting out for you! Write down your dreams and how you will use those dreams to glorify God. Then put in an action plan and figure out how to make your dreams a reality!

Prayer:

Dear Lord, I know I may be having a hard time accepting what I am being called to do, but I just ask if you will help me realize that you are in control and all things are possible through you. In Jesus' name I pray. Amen!

Withering beauty

Will your beauty be destroyed?
Written by Heather Hart

For the sun rises with scorching heat and withers the plant; its blossom falls and its beauty is destroyed.
~James 1:11

A lot of girls today put tons of time and effort into their appearances, more so than on any other area of their life. God's Word tells us that external beauty doesn't last forever. Even if you are the prettiest girl in your high school, external beauty will only get you so far. We need to remember that our true beauty comes not from what is outside, but from what is within us. Our internal beauty can never fade away or disappear, but grows and blossoms more beautifully with each passing year. In order for our inner beauty to grow, we have to spend time nourishing it. You know all of that time we spend making sure that our external appearance is up to par? What if we spent the same amount of time on our internal beauty? What if we spent that time reading our Bibles, praying, or worshiping God?

We have to be aware that our external beauty lasts only for a moment. Does it really matter if we are the prettiest girl at school? Probably not. Will our external appearance get us our dream job? It depends on what our dream job is, but probably not. Do we really want to marry the guy that is only dating us because he thinks we're hott? No. Yet there we are in front of the mirror each morning nit picking our external appearance, while ignoring our inner beauty, the beauty that really matters. Our internal beauty is what we hope our future husbands are attracted to. Our inner beauty will be what is remembered by our high school friends. And our internal state is what determines where we spend eternity; after all, our inner beauty comes from Christ, and without Him nothing else matters.

While we know that our external beauty will wither with old age and eventually be destroyed, we can also know that even if we live to be over 100 years old, we can radiate our internal beauty for the world to see, if we are willing to put the effort into it and let Christ transform us into His likeness.

Reflection:

Do you put more value into your outward appearance, expecting to live life one your external fading beauty, or on your inner, lasting beauty.

Application Step:

For the next week, make the commitment to spend as much time on your inner beauty as you do on your external appearance.

Prayer:

Father God, I need you. I tend to spend too much time on my external beauty, and put more value on it then I do on my true beauty. Please forgive me for elevating myself over you. Help me to put my external appearance into proper context, and help me to make you my top priority in my life, Lord. I beg you to work inside of me and transform me into your likeness. Help my personality to reflect you. I want to be beautiful on the inside and show others how wonderful you are. Thank you, Father, for all that you do for me. Thank you for showing me my faults, and for guiding me through this life. Thank you for never abandoning me, but for always being there with me to help me learn new things and get through the difficult times. Amen.

Friendships

What kind of friendship are you in?

Written by Caroline Sumner

There we found some brothers who invited us to spend a week with them...

~Acts 28:14

As teen girls, we have many friends. Some of our friendships are true friendships, while others are tools of Satan. We need to recognize which ones are which. Our true friends will be there no matter what. They will encourage us, but also tell us when we are in sin. Friendships that are tools of Satan will encourage us to sin, beat us down, and only be there for us when it's convenient for them. We are close to some friends, while other friends we aren't so close with, but the bottom line is that we should be nice to everyone. We should talk to all of our friends about God, and hopefully help them overcome and defeat Satan if we need to. We should never be rude or disrespectful to our classmates, even if they aren't our friends, because if they are Christians we should know that they are our brothers and sisters in Christ.

Reflection:

Do you respect people who aren't so close to you, or do you ignore them? Could you be a defeater of Satan through your friends?

Application Step:

Today take some time and socialize with some of your classmates that you aren't so close with, maybe even sit next to them at lunch. Be sure to talk about Christ, and share your faith with them.

Prayer:

Dear Lord, Please help me defeat Satan through my friends. Help me focus on you, and which of my friends have you living inside of them. Help me to be close to all my friends, and be a true friend for them. Help me to lift them up, use me to draw them closer to you, and please don't let me be a tool of Satan. In Jesus' name I pray. Amen.

Forgiveness

What about forgiveness?

Written by Heather Hart

Be kind and compassionate to one another, forgiving each other, just as in Christ God forgave you.
~Ephesians 4:32

This morning someone came to me and confessed something to me. They told me something that they did that hurt me a lot. I'm not going to tell you that I instantly forgave them, because I didn't. It took a bit for me to process what they had said, and then I had to choose how to respond. I could have responded with anger and resentment, but I chose not to. While their sin hurt me, God's Word says that we should forgive one another and be kind and compassionate. That isn't always easy, but we can do it. There have been many times in my life where I haven't responded this way, and I'm sure that you can think of some in your life too. Maybe when you found out that your best friend got the role in the school play that you wanted, or when your sister 'borrowed' your favorite shirt without asking and ruined it, or maybe when your boyfriend broke up with or cheated on you. The list could go on, there are so many times in life that we get hurt and our sinful human response is anger and resentment. We just want someone to be mad at, but that isn't what God wants from us. He wants us to be kind, compassionate, and forgive others, just as He forgave us. And the best part is that He is willing to help us do it. All we have to do is ask.

Reflection:

Is there anyone in your life that you need to forgive? Do you need to ask their forgiveness in return for responding initially with anger and resentment instead of kindness and compassion?

Application Step:

Ask God to help you forgive those who sin against, and pray that He helps you respond better in the future to bad situations. Do your best to treat everyone with kindness and compassion, and forgive those who sin against you.

Prayer:

Father God, I know that I am far from perfect, but I am ever so thankful that you chose to forgive me for my sins. Thank you, Lord. I pray now that you help me to show others the same kindness, compassion, and forgiveness that you have shown to me. I can't do that on my own, Father. I just can't. It's hard to look past the initial hurt, but with your help, I know that all things are possible. Please help me to treat others the way that you have treated me. In the name of your holy and precious Son, Jesus Christ, who died for the sins of the world, I pray. Amen.

One of a Kind

You were made to be somebody!
Written by Ashley McCollough

For we are God's workmanship, created in Christ Jesus to do good works, which God prepared in advance for us to do.
~Ephesians 2:10

Do you ever feel worthless, hopeless, unappreciated? I think we all feel this way at some point in our lives when we struggle with situations that are beyond our control. As girls we seem to hold on to more things than we should; with all the hate in the world, it's kinda hard not to. We get caught up in our flaws and what we can't do, or what we can't be...Sound familiar? Of course it does, every girl goes through this it's part of this crazy misunderstood life that we take in from the start. Many girls have cut themselves, or committed suicide because they felt like there was no point in living this life, that they didn't have the chances that you have. But it's simply isn't true! You were made to be somebody, whether it's a doctor, singer, writer, or even the president! All those things are very important and are great opportunities, but the most important thing is to always work for the glory of God. That means you have a life to live, a life to live for God. Even though you might not understand at first who God wants you to be, you can start off by being a great Christian, not just towards your family and friends, but all people. It is very easy to slip away from what God has to say and start looking at what others say; but you are NOT worthless, hopeless, or unappreciated. You are one of a kind, created by the most wonderful glorious person that ever walked this earth!

Reflection:

Are you struggling with doubt, thinking that you are a 'nobody', or are you going to be somebody that lives their life for God?

Application Step:

Look for more ways to honor God! Whether it is helping out at church or just helping a friend, be who God wants you to be, because you were born to be somebody!

Prayer:

Dear Heavenly Father, I just ask you to please help me through all the lies this world is telling me. Help me focus more on you, and what you want me to be and do. Help me to realize that I was born to be somebody wonderful that will do glorious works unto you, and to live my life according to your plan that you have set out for me. In Jesus name I pray. Amen!

Behavior

What does your behavior reflect?

Written by Heather Hart

To fear the LORD is to hate evil; I hate pride and arrogance, evil behavior and perverse speech.
~Proverbs 8:13

Our words and actions should reflect our fear of the Lord. This isn't the kind of fear that has us cowering in a corner, but the kind that we have for authority figures. It is the kind of fear that accompanies respect. When we respect people we don't want to offend them, we don't want them to look down on us, we desire them to look favorably on us as well. That's the kind of fear we should have for the Lord. When we have the healthy fear, we want the same things that He wants. Our actions should reflect that fear. We should hate the things He hates, and love the things He loves. When we know that He hates pride and arrogance, evil behavior and perverse speech, we should as well. But do we? Sometimes we love ourselves more than we love Christ. We love fun, even if it isn't good, clean fun, but fun that is harmful and sinful. When we choose to behave or hangout with people who are behaving in ways that the Lord hates, we aren't showing any kind of fear, respect, or love for Him. In fact, the Bible tells us that anyone who does evil hates light (John 3:20), and Jesus is the light of the world (John 8:12)...

Reflection:

What do your actions say about your relationship with Christ?

Application Step:

Pay attention to how you act. Make a conscious effort to change any actions that do not reflect fear of the Lord.

Prayer:

Lord God Almighty, I pray that you move in my life. Please, Lord, show me any actions or words that are part of my life that do not reflect my fear of you. I pray that you help me to love you more, and through that love, help me to reflect you. In the name of Jesus Christ I pray. Amen.

Anchored

What is your anchor?

Written by Shelley Hitz

We have this hope as an anchor for the soul, firm and secure...
~Hebrews 6:19

I'm a very visual person and I visualize this verse, this anchor to my soul, keeping me stable and firm. I visualize storms coming against me trying to knock me over, trying to weigh me down and get me to give in or compromise. All these things are constantly coming against me and, yet, I'm anchored. My soul is anchored firm secure and my hope is in Jesus Christ.

My husband and I went to Traverse City, Michigan, last weekend. It's right there at a bay and the weather was beautiful. The sun was shining off the water. In Traverse City, the water is a Caribbean blue color when the sun shines on it a certain way. We enjoyed sitting quietly and watching the water. As we were sitting there last night, we were watching a boat which had been anchored in the water. There was some choppy water and the boat was rocking to and fro, but it never moved its position because it was anchored.

I encourage you if you have true beauty in Christ, if you have a relationship in Christ, then your soul, your hope can be anchored in Jesus Christ. You don't have to be swayed to and fro. You don't have to be swayed by what your friends say or what your boyfriend thinks of you or what the mirror says back to you. You can be anchored because we have this hope in Jesus Christ as an anchor for the soul, firm and secure.

Reflection:

Are you anchored by hope in Jesus Christ, or are the winds of life blowing you out to sea?

Application Step:

~If you haven't already accepted Jesus Christ as your anchor of hope, find a Christian and talk with them about how to do so.

~If you do have Jesus as your anchor of hope, look up the following Scriptures from Psalm and memorize one:
- Psalm 25:5
- Psalm 31:24
- Psalm 39:7
- Psalm 42:11
- Psalm 62:5
- Psalm 71:14

Prayer:

Father God, I am so thankful for you, oh Lord. I am thankful to have you as my anchor. I am so grateful that I can put my hope in you no matter what I am going through. I am thankful that you are trustworthy. I'm thankful that as long as my hope is in you, it doesn't matter how strong any of the storms of this life are, you will keep me safe in the harbor of your love. Thank you. In the name of your son, Jesus Christ, I pray. Amen.

Casting Stones

Are you selfish with grace?

Written by Heather Hart

Why do you look at the speck of sawdust in your brother's eye and pay no attention to the plank in your own eye?

~Luke 6:41

It is so easy to see when other people are screwing up. We could sit there all day and point out flaws in other people's actions, especially those of other Christians. However, that isn't what God wants from us. I love that Jesus, the only perfect person to ever walk the face of the earth didn't do that. He could have. He is the only one who has ever had the right to cast stones, yet instead, He gave His life for us, so that we could be forgiven. But we don't offer grace like that. We are certainly happy to receive God's grace. We are thankful that He is so gracious towards us, but then we sit there and look down on others. We judge them because we don't think that they dress the right way, or talk the right way. We stick our noses up at others because we don't think that they are as good as we are, or worthy of our attention. I don't know about you, but I am certainly thankful that Jesus didn't treat us that way.

Unlike Jesus, who was perfect in every way, we are sinners. We sin every single day in some way or another. You don't believe me? 1 John 1 says that if we say we have not sinned we make Christ out to be a lair, and if we say that there is no sin in us we deceive ourselves. We sin; all of us, each and every one of us sin. But instead of working through our own salvation, we focus on the sins of others. After all, that makes us feel a whole lot better, but it isn't what God wants from us. He doesn't want us to hoard His grace all to ourselves, but to show that same grace to others. Jesus didn't die for our sins alone, but for the sins of the world. That includes the lady at church who looks down on the high school kids for one reason or another. That includes the sins of your best friend, even if they are sins against you. It includes the sins of our parents, of our peers, teachers, and family twice removed.

Reflection:

Do you offer the same grace to others as God has offered to you? Or are you busy casting stones and worrying about their saw dust, while you are blinded by the plank?

Application Step:

Every time you catch yourself judging someone, compliment them on something that they do well. Even if it is someone clear across the room, walk over and compliment them. If it is someone who you aren't with, pick up a phone and call them just to tell them something nice.

Prayer:

Father God, I am so selfish with your grace! Please forgive me. I have been casting stones and pointing out sawdust all the while with a plank in my own eye. Help me to encourage others, even in my thoughts. Help me to focus on my own sins, and grow closer to you. My walk with you is the only one that I have control over, so help me to focus my thoughts on sharing your grace, and growing in my love for you. In the name of your Son I pray. Amen.

Anxiety

What's your outlet?
Written by Shelley Hitz

Cast all your anxiety on him because he cares for you.
~1 Peter 5:7

You know, there are a lot of things in life that can cause anxiety. It may be different for each of us. I know one thing for me that causes anxiety at times is uncertainty, not knowing what's going to happen, not knowing what the future holds, and it may be different things for you. It may be a competition that you are in or a test that is coming up or relationship issues with your friends or your parents. There are a lot of things in life that can cause anxiety.

I was reading something the other day and they gave a picture of what anxiety can be like, it really caught my attention and I thought I would share it with you. They said anxiety is kind of like holding a hand grenade and on that hand grenade you pull that pin. Within time, it is going to go off. You are, basically, holding it and it is either going to do damage to you or you can throw it away from you. If you throw it in the direction of other people, it can hurt them and damage them, or you can choose to throw it as far away from you and anyone else as possible so that no one gets hurt. Now, if you were really in true life having a hand grenade that the pin was pulled and you knew it was just going to be seconds before it went, you would get rid of it. You would throw it away. You would get it away from you and anyone else as quickly as you could.

But, so many times in life we hold on to that anxiety. We allow it to just fester, go off, and cause damage. Or, we allow it to roll and roll around in our heads or we give it to other people. Maybe we get angry at someone and allow that anxiety to cause hurt and pain in someone else's life. I thought that was a great picture of just casting it away and throwing it away as far away from us and others as we can.

In I Peter 5:7, it says, "Cast all your anxiety on Him because He cares for you." Jesus wants to take on our anxiety. He is there. He can handle it. He can detonate the bomb, so to speak. He knows what to do with it and He is the one who can handle it.

Reflection:

Do you have any anxiety that you need to let go of? Are you going to hold onto it until it hurts yourself or those around you, or will you cast it upon Christ?

Application Step:

Don't hold on to anxiety anymore. Cast it upon Him because he cares for you.

Prayer:

Father God, I have a tendency to hang onto anxiety. I have a tendency to hold onto it until I end up hurting myself or others. Please help me to cast my anxiety on you, oh Lord. Help me to surrender my anxiety bomb to you, before I hurt someone. Help me to trust you, Lord. Help me to understand that you are capable of handling all of my problems, and I need not be anxious when my hope and trust are in you. Thank you, Father, for the peace that you give. Thank you for taking my anxiety. In the name of your Son, Amen.

All Powerful

Our great and mighty God...
Written by Ashley McCollough

I know that the LORD is great, that our Lord is greater than all gods.

~Psalm 135:5

The power of God is above everything, the strength that He holds is very hard to comprehend and compare to our lives. We face struggles everyday that may seem to overpower us throughout our day, or maybe our lives, but nothing can compare to the power of God. He knows what will happen tomorrow, next week, and even next year; He knows all. He has shown His strength and power throughout the Bible with the wonderful miracles He performed, that no one could do except God Himself, and He wants you to know that whatever struggle you are facing in life, and it just seems so hard to bear, always remember ask for God's help. He will willingly take all the weight off your shoulders that you're carrying around with you that you probably don't need. God wants you to be able to come to Him with your problems, because He defiantly wants to help you in whatever way He can. You are His child. So always remember to give it all to God, because He is powerful enough to handle anything.

Reflection:

Are you giving it all to God, or are you carrying around that extra weight?

Application Step:

Today ask God to help lift all that weight off your shoulders, and know God is all powerful.

Prayer:

Dear Lord, I just ask if you will please help me in whatever struggles I am dealing with at the moment. Help me be able to see that you are all powerful, and that you can handle anything. I just give all these problems to you, and know that everything is going to be taken care of. Thank you for everything you have done. In Jesus name I pray. Amen!

Unpleasant Circumstances

Can you see the good through the bad?
Written by Heather Hart

Surely your goodness and love will follow me all the days of my life, and I will dwell in the house of the LORD forever.
~Psalm 23:6

This week my family has been going through some really rough times. I am so thankful for God's Word during times like these. The above verse has really been speaking to me today. David wrote that goodness and love would FOLLOW us, not lead us. While we go through things that are unpleasant, or seem to be devastating, we can trust that God's goodness and love are following us. He is with us, and He can use ALL things together for the good of those that love Him and are called according to His purpose (Romans 8:28).

While I might be going through a tough time, I know that it won't last forever. I can take heart knowing that while in this world I have troubles, Jesus has overcome the world (John 16:33). I know that God loves me no matter what, and He loves you too. While life isn't always a bed of roses, I trust that something good comes out of every situation. Thus, goodness follows us.

It's sometimes easier to focus on the situation at hand, the devastating news, or the unpleasant circumstances, but when we look forward to see what God can do through the situation, everything becomes more tolerable. When I look back on life I realize that some of the worst times during my life brought about the best things in my life now. Goodness has always followed me, even when I thought my life was ending. My guess is that the same is true for you. You just might not realize it yet.

Reflection:

Are you focusing on the unpleasant situation you are in, or are you looking forward to see how God might be using this for good?

Application Step:

Read the story of Joseph (Genesis 37 and Genesis 50:20) Look back over your life and identify some good things that have came from seemingly bad situations.

Prayer:

Lord God, Sometimes it just feels like my life is falling apart. The world seems to come crashing down on me, and I just can't see anything good. Help me, Lord. Help me to see how you bring good things from bad situations. Help me to see the goodness that is following me. I know that you are always with me, God. And I trust that you can use all things for good, please, help me to be able to see the good you are doing. In Jesus name I pray. Amen.

God's Glory

Let's accessorize!
Written by Shelley Hitz

And we, who with unveiled faces all reflect the Lord's glory, are being transformed into his likeness with ever-increasing glory, which comes from the Lord, who is the Spirit.
~2 Corinthians 3:18

Have you ever found yourself comparing your appearance to others, or have you ever felt 'less than' as you look at what other people are wearing. Well, I have to admit there are days I still struggle with this. Although God has freed me from so much, and helped me to find my true beauty in Christ, there are still moments that I struggle. One of those moments happened recently when I had the opportunity to speak at a teen girl conference in the Bahamas, (yes, that's right, I was "suffering" for Jesus in the Bahamas). It was an amazing time. I went with a ministry called, Get Real in Christ, and was working and serving alongside teen girls and women. They were beautiful women from the inside and outside. These teen girls had a heart for Jesus that was just amazing.

One of our last days there was a Sunday and we were getting ready for church. I had just thrown a bunch of clothes into a suitcase and most of them I had planned on leaving for the people there. I usually do that when I go on mission trips. So, I didn't really have a good outfit combination for church that Sunday. As I was looking at my options I thought, oh, man, I am going to look really plain. You know, everyone else was wearing dresses and skirts, and cute combinations of clothes and I just kind of sat in front of the mirror and thought, oh, I just look plain. I was thinking should I ask if I can borrow somebody's jewelry or someone's accessories.

Then, all of a sudden, not in an audible voice but in my heart, I felt like the Lord said, "Shelley, you have My glory as your accessory." I was like, oh, really? Oh my goodness, I didn't even think about that - having God's glory as my accessory, having Him in my life radiating out through me, having Christ in me as my true beauty. That is my best accessory. Wow! That was a different way to look at it. All of a sudden I was okay. You know, I still had those moments, but I was reminding myself that my accessory is God's glory - that sparkle that shines out through my eyes, the smile that sends the message of God's love to those I meet.

I like this verse in 2 Corinthians 3: 18. It says, "And we, who with unveiled faces, all reflect the Lord's glory are being transformed into His likeness with ever increasing glory which comes from the Lord who is the spirit." Because we do; we reflect the Lord's glory. When we have a relationship with Jesus and He lives in us, we reflect Him.

Reflection:

Have you remembered to put on your most important accessory this morning: a relationship with Jesus that will reflect His glory to others?

Application Step:

Be sure to spend time in prayer and reading God's Word each day this week. If you don't already have a Bible reading plan, read a Psalm a day.

Prayer:

Lord, Thank you for being the most beautiful thing in my life. I ask that you help me to remember that nothing I own could ever compare to your glory. When I start to compare myself to others, remind me that I have you, there is nothing in this world that I should ever be jealous of. In Jesus' name I pray. Amen.

Equal

Is that the same difference or no difference?

Written by Heather Hart

There is neither Jew nor Gentile, neither slave nor free, nor is there male and female, for you are all one in Christ Jesus.
~Galatians 3:28

God's Word tells us that He sees us all the same. He doesn't care if we are Hispanic, Caucasian, or Chinese. He doesn't care if you are popular or unpopular. He doesn't categorize us by the grades we get or the style of clothes we wear. He just loves us, all of us.

We can be encouraged by that, but we can also be challenged by it. We can be encouraged to know that He loves us the same as He loves the straight 'A' students, that girl at church that can recite Bible verses all day long without batting an eye, and He loves us as much as He loves our friends, families and church leaders. That is encouraging! However, it gets challenging when we realize that He loves others as much as He loves us. He loves the kid at school that is cheating, but still getting the same grades as you. He loves the girl that the guy you have a crush on is dating, and He loves EVERYONE just as much as He loves us. We are all equal in His eyes. He loves us all the same. That means that Christ died for their sins as well as ours. He doesn't differentiate between the rich and the poor, the smart and the not so smart, or even between the church members and people that have never heard of Him.

So my question to you is, if God loves us all equally, can we love everyone else that way? Can we put aside our differences and love everyone God created? That doesn't mean we have to love their sins, and most certainly doesn't mean that we should encourage them to sin, but can we love them despite their sins? After all, God loves us despite our sins...

Reflection:

Do you love everyone despite their sins, status and level of knowledge or physical ability, or do you harbor hatred for the people that God created?

Application Step:

Find some way to show love to someone you normally wouldn't. Be creative!

Prayer:

Father God, Thank you for loving me. Help me to love others the way that you love them. You love us all despite our sins, but I tend to hold peoples sins against them, I hold their status of living against them, and I hold their amount of knowledge against them. Please help me to look past all of those things, and love them. Help me to love them because you created them. In the name of Christ Jesus I pray. Amen.

Peer Pressure

What kind of pressure are you getting?

Written by Shelley Hitz

For where two or three come together in my name, there am I with them."

~Matthew 18:20

Have you ever felt pressured into doing something? Well, there's the term "peer pressure". Most of the time we hear it in the negative connotation, like negative peer pressure with your friends wanting you to drink or wanting you to give in to having sex or something like that. But, there is also positive peer pressure.

The other day I went running where I was planning to go running with a group. We have a group close to our home that we run with on Thursday nights. My husband is the runner. He runs well, he runs fast, and he runs consistently. I'm just an occasional runner. I just do it to stay in shape. But, I decided to go along with him this night. It just so happens that as we were getting ready to run, it started pouring down rain. I'm not talking about sprinkling. I'm talking about pouring down rain! I was standing there and had a decision to make. Either, I was going to go out and run like I planned to do or I would stay back and wait for the group to come back. Well, that night anyone who ran got a pair of free socks. There was all this positive peer pressure because everybody was going to go out and run. I could stay back or I could go. I finally gave in to the peer pressure and ran. Now that night, it was positive peer pressure because it got me to go out and exercise and do something that I probably wouldn't have done otherwise. It wasn't lighting or thundering. It wasn't going to put any harm to me to go out there and run. It was summer, so it wasn't anything harmful - it was positive peer pressure from the group. Everyone who was going to go do it, encouraged me to run.

You know what? We need people in our lives spiritually who can encourage us. The Bible says where two or three are gathered, Jesus is there. The Holy Spirit is there. So, it's important that we have people around us who can provide that positive peer pressure.

I want to ask you. Do you have people in your life, in your school and close friends who are following Christ who are really seeking to find their true beauty in Christ and are seeking to find their value and worth in Christ? Because if you don't, I encourage you to start praying for God to provide someone for you. It really does make a difference whether or not you're surrounding yourself with people who are going to pressure you into doing things negatively.

Reflection:

Do you have that negative peer pressure, or do you have people who are going to support you and help you to do those things that Christ is calling us to do, in following and hearing His voice and obeying Him?

Application Step:

I encourage you to find people who will help you give in to positive peer pressure if you don't already have it. If you do, thank those who provide it.

Prayer:

Father God, You amaze me. Thank you for using others to encourage me. I ask that you strengthen those in my life that provide positive peer pressure, and bring even more people into my life that will encourage me to follow you. I also ask, Lord, that you use me to encourage others, and provide positive peer pressure in their lives. In the name of Christ I pray. Amen.

Challenge

Are you up for it?

Written by Heather Hart

"In everything I did, I showed you that by this kind of hard work we must help the weak, remembering the words the Lord Jesus himself said: 'It is more blessed to give than to receive.'"

~Acts 20:35

God's Word tells us that it is better to give than to receive, and let me tell you, giving to others always makes me feel good. It's just such a great feeling providing for someone's need, or just blessing them in some way. It can also provide an opportunity to tell them about Christ. It's just one of the many ways that we can bring glory to His name.

There are sometimes that God asks us to give certain things, like with the rich young ruler (Mark 10:17-23). He asks that because there are things that we tend to love more than God. For this young man, he loved his wealth more than he loved God. He wasn't willing to give it up for Christ. So, Jesus instructed the rich young ruler to sell everything he owned and give it to the poor. Can you imagine how that ruler must have felt? Can you imagine God asking the same thing from you? Would you be willing to do as Jesus asked? Well, the good news is that you don't have to sell everything that you own to be a follower of Christ (although some people do). However, God does expect His people to care for those less fortunate (and trust me, no matter how unfortunate you are, there is always someone who is less fortunate). The way this plays out in our lives varies from person to person. As teenagers, it might not feel like we can do a whole lot to help others, but that simply isn't true. Helping others can be as simple as visiting a nursing home, donating your old clothes to Good Will, or even helping someone else with their homework. Everyone has someone to offer.

Reflection:

How can you help someone in need? What are your strong points? What do you have to offer others?

Application Step:

I challenge you to find some way to give to the poor. You can take part in the true beauty challenge on our website (http://www.teen-beauty-tips.com/true-beauty-challenge.html) or come up with an idea of your own. Be sure and tell us about it!

Prayer:

Lord, Thank you for giving me the opportunity to help others. Please show me how you can use me to bless those around me. Help me to see ways, even small ways, that I can help people that are within my reach. I know I can't change the world, but I can do your work where I am. I want to do my part to share your love. In the name of Jesus Christ, my Lord and Savior, I pray. Amen.

Security Tag

Paid in full!

Written by Shelley Hitz

I tell you the truth, you will not get out until you have paid the last penny.

~Matthew 5:26

Have you been shopping lately? Well, if you have you will know what I mean when I say security tag. They are those tags put on clothes in the store to keep you from walking out with them. They are kind of like a plastic piece attached to your pants or your sweater or the things which are usually more expensive. Let's say you go to that store, you put on a pair of pants that has a security tag on it and you walk out of the store. What is going to happen? An alarm is going to go off, right? It is going to alert the store and the security staff that somebody is trying to steal something from their store. Who is the only person who can take that security tag off? If you try to take it off yourself in the dressing room, what is probably going to happen to those pants? They are probably going to get ripped or some of the security tags even have a way where ink comes out of them and could stain your pants. It is probably going to ruin them. So you have to take them to the cashier and pay your money. Then, the clerk has that little device and can pop off that tag and you are good to go.

Well, let's just say that security tag represents sin. Sin is the way we have missed God's mark, so to speak, in our lives.

The stuff we have done or the stuff which has been done against us. To know what sin is, you can just take a quick look at the Ten Commandments and see what God's standards are: "You shall not lie." Have you ever told a lie? "Don't steal." Have you ever stolen something, even something really small? The list goes on and on and they even talk about not committing adultery. Well, Jesus talked about even if you lust after someone in your heart you have committed adultery with them in your heart. I know for me I have committed all of those. I was caught stealing a tube of lipstick when I was in high school. Yes, not cars, not anything big, not jewelry or anything, I was trying to steal a tube of lipstick. One of those undercover cop-type people who looks for shoplifters during the holiday season caught me and I got in trouble for it. You may have stolen something small, or maybe something big, but I think if we are honest we have all sinned in some way. You could imagine that we are walking around with that security tag of sin on us.

Now, who is the only person who can take that sin from us? The Bible says that the only one who can take our sin from us is Jesus. No other religion, nothing we do, no amount of good works can get rid or take off that sin from us. Jesus has come to forgive us of that sin. If we try to get rid of it on our own, we are probably going to make a mess, because we just can't do it. We need Jesus. So, someday we are going to face what is called, "Judgment Day". We are going to face Christ and have to answer to Him for what we have done while in the body whether good or bad. If we go up there with our sin with that "security tag" and we walk through the gates of heaven what is going to happen? An alarm is going to go off, so to speak. God is going to know that we have that sin and that we are carrying that sin with us. But, if we come to Him this side of heaven and we are truly repentant, we have realized the ways that we have done wrong against God and we are sorry for that and we repent of those sins, not just saying we want to do different but actually through Christ's power doing different. Our life changes. We have a hunger for God, for His Word, for doing what He has commanded us. We have His love, His Holy Spirit that is in us; His love, His joy, His peace. It is not going to be an instant thing, but we begin to change.

Psalm 130:3-4 says, "If you, oh Lord, kept a record of sins, oh Lord who could stand." That is how I feel today. I wouldn't be able to stand. Then, it goes on and says, "…but with You, there is forgiveness. Therefore, You are feared." 1 John 1:9 says, "If we confess our sins, He is faithful and just and will forgive us our sins and purify us from all unrighteousness." In Hebrews 10:17, God says, "Their sins and lawless acts I will remember no more."

Reflection:

Are you trying to take off your security tag on your own? Or are you allowing Jesus to pay for your sins and take that security tag off of you?

Application Step:

If you haven't accepted the blood of Jesus as the payment for your sins, seek out someone who you can speak with to learn more.

If you have, praise God for sending Jesus Christ to remove your security tag of sin. If there are any sins that you haven't asked Him to forgive, ask Him now. Acknowledge the fact that there is nothing you can do to take off that security tag, that you need Him in your life.

Prayer:

Father God, Thank you so much for sending Jesus to pay for my sin, and then remove it from me. I'm so thankful that I don't have it stuck to me for all of eternity. I could have never paid for my sins on my own, Lord. I know that. Thank you so much for providing the payment so that my sin could be removed from me. Thank you for submitting payment for me, and letting me know that the price of my sin has been paid in full! In the name of my redeemer I pray. Amen.

Hunger

The sweet stuff of the world
Written by Shelley Hitz

He who is full loathes honey, but to the hungry even what is bitter tastes sweet.

~Proverbs 27:7

Recently, I was on a retreat and while I was there I decided to just fast one day. I was just going to eat fruits and vegetables. I was doing that so I could really pray and seek God in some things in my life. So, that day I was simply eating fruits and vegetables-no sweets, no anything. The last couple of days before that, to be honest, I over-indulged in some sweets. One day I bought some Reese's cups. It was perhaps a pack of ten and I think I probably ate almost the whole pack. It was that bad. Then, the next day someone had given me two little cupcake-sized things of cheesecake. Well, they were pretty rich and I ate both of them in one sitting. I had just over-indulged in sweets and I needed a break from it anyway.

That day I was fasting and I was just eating fruits and vegetables, but I was thinking, man, oh, if only I could have some chocolate or only if I could have some cheesecake. I was hungry for those things. Since I wasn't eating those things for the whole day when it came time to eat I made myself a fruit salad of oranges, blueberries, apples and put some other stuff in. Then, oh my goodness it tasted so sweet! You know why? Because I was not giving myself the artificial stuff, the junk.

The sweet stuff and the real sugar, the real stuff from the fruit, tasted so good.

It made me think of our spiritual lives and how many times we get full on the sweet things of the world - the stuff that the world says is so good, the media, movies, television shows, music, internet, Facebook, and just on and on and on. We can get full of that stuff to when we then go to read our Bible or we go to pray it is like it's boring. It isn't fun. This isn't cool. I want more of that television show, I want to watch another movie or I want to play a video game. So, it reminded me of how when I didn't eat and didn't get full on all the sweet stuff, that the fruit tasted so much better. The real sugar, the real stuff, that God has intended for our bodies to have. It is so much better for us. It tasted so good. In Proverbs 27:7, it says, "He who is full loathes honey but to the hungry, even what is bitter tastes sweet." So, if you have ever had a meal, you are so full at the restaurant and then the waitress comes up and asks you, "Do you want dessert?" You are so full you are like, no, I couldn't eat another thing! That is what this verse is talking about. He who is full loathes honey so he doesn't even want the sweet things of the world. To the hungry, to those who are really hungry, even what is bitter tastes sweet because you are so hungry, you are so famished that anything tastes good at that time.

Reflection:

Are you filling yourself full with the junk food and the sweet things of the world? So even the sweet things of God and the stuff that is intended to help you grow and to give you life and life to the full that stuff you don't even want it any more. It is not even interesting to you. Or, are you allowing God to give you wisdom on how to walk through this life and navigate all your media choices and the things you are doing so you are not full on the things of the world. Are you able to clear your life, clear your schedule or clear the stuff that is going on to where you can leave some room for God?

Application Step:

Just come to Him. Turn your phone off if you need to. Just focus on Him – journal or pray or go on a walk. Just be in nature with God. Being in a relationship with Jesus is one of the most rewarding, satisfying, exciting things that has ever happened to me, but it has taken time for me to really come to Him and be able to receive that from Him. There were so many other things blocking it out. I encourage you to taste the sweetness of Christ today. Make room in your life for Him.

Prayer:

Father God, I have been filling up on the sweet things of this world, and not being hungry enough from you. The things of this world, Lord, I know they aren't good for me. The food that I get from you, God, that is the good stuff. Help me to be hungry for you. Help me to set aside the time I need to soak you in. In the name of Jesus I pray. Amen.

Wake Up!

Did you turn your alarm on?

Written by Shelley Hitz

The hour has come for you to wake up from your slumber, because our salvation is nearer now than when we first believed.

~Romans 13:11

Have you ever set your alarm the night before school or work or something like that and then realize you set the time but you never turned the alarm on? Oh my goodness! I have done this several times lately and I don't know what I'm thinking. I set my alarm; I think I'm all set for the day; and then when it comes around I am not waking up at the right time because I didn't turn it on. This happened the other day for work. I was working for the hospital that day as a physical therapist and I needed to be at work at 6 a.m. sharp. That is pretty early and I don't normally wake up on my own so I set the alarm and went to sleep. Well, what did I do? I didn't turn the alarm on! So, I turned over and am thinking oh, wow, I feel really rested like I got a lot of sleep. All of a sudden I look at my alarm clock and it says 5:45. I need to be at work in 15 minutes! I jump out of bed and rush around. Thankfully, I didn't have to wash my hair and get a shower that day so I could hurry and get ready real quickly. I already had my lunch packed and out so I was able to get to work (I only live a few minutes away) and actually clock in to work with one minute to spare. Now, if I wouldn't have made it to work on time or if I would have overslept I would have gotten what is called "an occurrence." After you get so many occurrences you can get fired. So, this was a fairly big deal. I needed to be at work on time.

I just want to ask you something today. I'm wondering if you need to wake up spiritually, so to speak. Maybe you set your alarm. You know, you're going to church, you're going to youth group, every once in a while you crack open your Bible and you think you're okay. You think you are ready. You think you are ready for that day when Jesus comes back. That day they call "Judgment Day" when He will take those to heaven with Him, those who have a relationship with Him. But maybe you're just going through the motions or maybe you are just doing it for your friends or your parents. Maybe you have never truly asked Christ to come into your life. Maybe you have never truly repented. So, you think your "alarm" is on. You think you have done the things you need to do. You're a fairly good person, according to what you think, but you are really not ready. When that day comes, you could be awoken with an alarm and your spirit saying, oh no, I am not ready. Unlike my story, I was still able to make it. You know, you may not make it if you don't prepare now. So, what have you done with Jesus? Who is He in your life?

Jesus said of Himself, "I am the way, the truth and the life. No one comes to the Father except through Me." That is in John 14:6. Then, in Acts 4:12, Peter, filled with the Holy Spirit, said, "It is by the name of Jesus Christ of Nazareth whom you crucified but whom God raised from the dead that this man stands before you healed." Well, actually that was in verse 10, but he then goes on to say in verse 12, "Salvation is found in no one else. For there is no other name under heaven, given to men, by which we must be saved." Salvation is found in no one else or nothing else. Going to church is not going to make you saved. Going to a Christian school does not give you salvation. Reading your Bible, being in a Christian family, none of those things gives you salvation. You may think today that your alarm is set. You may think you are doing good, that you are set for the day Jesus comes back, but I encourage you today to take a long, hard look within yourself, to examine yourself and to see where you stand with Jesus. Do you truly know Him? Have you truly given your life to Him, surrendered everything to Him and truly repented? Not just say, oh, I want to do better but truly repented with your actions. Your life is going to be different. When you are a follower of Jesus and when you are finding your true beauty in Christ people are going to see the difference. They are going to see the change in your life.

Reflection:

Is your alarm set, but not on? Do you need to wake up spiritually, and truly give your life to Christ?

Application Step:

Set aside your 'good Christian' checklist for a moment and just spend some time with God. Examine your heart to see where you really stand with Him.

Prayer:

Lord God, I help me to see my true standing with you. I do not want to over sleep and miss your return. Help me to be awake spiritually. Help me to be alert, and keep my eyes on you, God. In the name of your son I pray. Amen.

Big Enough

Do you believe God brings good out of the bad?

Written by Sarah Louise

And we know that in all things God works for the good of those who love him, who have been called according to his purpose.

~ Romans 8:28

Life isn't perfect...bad things happen. Family members pass away, we lose friends, fights happen, and love sometimes hurts. We've all experienced those few hurtful words that sting and those arguments that stick with us. There are bad situations all over the world....kids starving, orphans without homes, parents who leave, rapes, and abusive homes. But can you ever imagine God can use those bad situations for good, for His glory?

From my own experiences I have seen God's light shine through every situation, good or bad. He showed me forgiveness through my parent's divorce, love through a bad breakup, and hope through my grandfather's death. We may not be able to the good He can bring in the midst of our problems, but we can trust that our God is big enough to bring the best out of the bad.

Reflection:

What situation are you in now? Do you truly believe God can use your pain for good?

Application Step:

Instead of freaking out or getting depressed because of your problems, write down the ways God could use your pain for good. You never know. He could use what you go through to touch someone else's life through your testimony.

Prayer:

Jesus, thank you for being the hope I can cling to in the midst of my storm. I know you can use this situation for good…I just need to trust you. Help me to look above my problems and to fix my eyes on you. I love you Lord. In your precious name I pray. Amen.

Intimidation

Power, love and self-discipline...
Written by Sondra Isbell

For God did not give us a spirit of timidity, but a spirit of power, of love and of self-discipline.

~2 Timothy 1:7

What are you intimidated by? Could it be your friends, family, guys, or money? The list can go on and on. Living under the weight of intimidation can keep you feeling confused, anxious, and sometimes alone. Relationships are often affected by what you let intimidate you. Intimidation is NOT a gift from God. In fact, the bible says --"I have not given you the spirit of timidity." You must learn to stir up the gifts God has placed inside of you, "power, love and self-discipline." I encourage you to stop feeling that you have to walk around always defeated and less of a person. God's power working through you will give you the knowledge you need to be able to face your giant of intimidation.

How do I break free of intimidation?

1). by asking: Matt. 7:8- "For everyone who asks receives; he who seeks finds; and to him who knocks, the door will be opened." So all you have to do is ASK.

2). by receiving: 1 Thess. 5:9- "For God did not appoint us to suffer wrath but to receive salvation through our Lord Jesus Christ." Just like you receive a birthday gift from your parents or a friend, you can do the same with God, but on a daily basis.

3). by believing: Phil. 4:13- "I can do everything through Him (Christ) who gives me strength." Not just one thing but everything; that means all things.

When you ask, receive and believe on what God has given you, you will then be better prepared for what God has for you. Your destiny doesn't consist of "intimidation" but boldness and power through what God has already given you.

Reflection:

Are you letting the things of this world intimidate you, or are you putting your trust in Christ?

Application Step:

Write down the things that intimidate you. After you have made your list, rip them up and throw them away. Then, memorize Philippians 4:13, "I can do everything through [Christ] who gives me strength."

Prayer:

Dear God, I thank you for all the gifts you have given me. Help me to know that I do have your strength working through me. Give me wisdom and knowledge everyday so that I will know what to do. Don't let me look at others, but keep my eyes on you!

Empty

Are you running on empty?

Written by Shelley Hitz

May the God of hope fill you with all joy and peace as you trust in Him, so that you may overflow with hope by the power of the Holy Spirit.

~Romans 15:13

Today, I want to share an embarrassing story with you. One week when my husband was out of town, I noticed on Monday that our truck was starting to run out of gas. It was pretty low and I needed to get it filled up, but one thing led to the other and I kept procrastinating. Well, you can only guess what happened to me on Wednesday after work. Yep, I ran out of gas. So I'm sitting at this stoplight getting ready to go when it turned green, and I had no gas. I was stuck. People are honking their horns like, 'Come on lady! Let's go!' and there's nothing that I could do. I could not move my vehicle. How embarrassing.

Well I want to ask you today, have you ever felt empty in your life (spiritually speaking)? Have you ever felt like you were stuck, so to speak? I believe that just as that gas tank is created to be filled with gas, we are vessels created to be filled with something. 2 Corinthians 4:7 tells us that we are vessels; we're a jar of clay. It say's: *but we have this treasure in jars of clay to show that this all-surpassing power is from God and not from us.*

We're not just designed to contain anything or just something, we're vessels designed to contain someone. We're not just vessels, we're actually temples. You see 1 Corinthians 6:19-20 says: *Do you not know that your body is a temple of the Holy Spirit, who is in you, whom you have received from God? You are not your own; you were bought at a price. Therefore honor God with your body.* What is the purpose of a temple? Well may I suggest to you that the purpose of the temple is to contain a god? And in our case as believers, as Christians, as Christ followers, we have been designed to contain the God of this universe, God Almighty.

I want to ask you, if you feel stuck today in your life, if you feel empty, if you feel like you're running on fumes, just barely surviving? Because I know I have been there before. If that's where you are, I want to encourage you to realize that just as I ran out of that gas on Wednesday, and was stuck, that when we try to do things on our own strength and in our own ways, when we try to find our true beauty on our own, we're going to reach a point where we are going to reach empty. We are designed to be vessels; just like that gas tank is designed to be filled with gas, we are designed to be filled with the Holy Spirit.

Reflection:

Is your tank full, or are you running on empty?

Application Step:

Fill up on God! Spend time reading your Bible, praying, and singing praise and worship songs.

Prayer:

Lord God, I come to you now feeling empty. I ask you to fill me with your Spirit, Lord. Remind me that I can't do everything on my own, but that you designed me to be full of you. Help me to find my true beauty in you, oh Lord. In the name of your precious and holy Son I pray. Amen.

Checklist

Are you trying to make it on your own?
Written by Heather Hart

This is love for God: to obey his commands. And his commands are not burdensome,
~1 John 5:3

The Bible has a lot of rules and guidelines. It contains instructions for being the perfect Christian. The only problem is that we aren't perfect people. We can try all we want to follow every little detail in the Bible, but at the end of each day, we will still fall short. We can have the desire to please God, but we are merely sinful humans. We can't achieve perfection here on earth, but the good news is that God knew that. He doesn't expect us to be perfect. That's why He sent His Son, Jesus Christ. He sent Jesus to live a life on earth, showing us how we should live to honor God, and then to die on the cross, because He knew we couldn't do it. I'm not saying that we shouldn't try to follow the Bible, what I am saying is that we can't earn our way to heaven. We can't earn God's love by doing what He says, because we already have it.

Our 'job' as Christians isn't to check off a list of things that we did or didn't do each day. It is simply to love Christ with all that we are. Once we put our faith in Christ, and declare Him as Lord over our lives, we are forgiven for being sinful humans. However, if we truly love Him, we will do our best to honor Him. Not to complete some check list, but because we love Him and want to do what He says. If we truly love Christ, we won't be looking at the impossible task before us and groaning because of all the things the Bible says to do or not to do. We will look ahead with joy at the chance for serving Christ. We won't be burdened by His commands, but be filled with peace knowing that while our task is impossible our God is full of grace, mercy, and forgiveness.

Reflection:

Are you putting marks on your 'good Christian' checklist, or are you living a life full of love for Christ?

Application Step:

When you are tempted to start checking off your 'good Christian' checklist, take a step back and remember that you are covered by grace, remember that it is impossible to earn forgiveness. Then, take a moment to thank God for sending Jesus to pay for your sinfulness, and move forward with a heart set on pleasing Christ, not on completing a 'to do' list.

Prayer:

Father God, your love amazes me. Thank you for sending your Son to die for my sinfulness. Thank you for forgiving me even though I will never live up to the standard that you set. Please help me to move forward not out of obligation, but out of love for you. Help me to want to live a life pleasing to you, but also help me to remember that that is an impossible task and that I need your grace, love and forgiveness every moment of every day. In the name of your Son, Jesus Christ, I pray. Amen.

Remembrance

How do you remember your Creator?
Written by Elissa Branum

Remember your Creator in the days of your youth, before the days of trouble come and the years approach when you will say, "I find no pleasure in them"— ...Then man goes to his eternal home and mourners go about the streets.
~Ecclesiastes 12:1, 5

It's obvious that this is not a very "feel good" verse, but it is truthful. My good friend shared it with me when we were discussing purity and a Biblical view on dating. Personally, I believe that God's will for my life is to not date/court until His time for me is revealed. That is my way of remembering Him in my youth and seeking what His desires are for my focus.

The author of Ecclesiastes throughout the book tells of how he has tried worldly pleasures but has found out, aside from God, "Everything is meaningless!" (Ecclesiastes 12:8). What we consider "fun" now will fade. Yet, every day we may feel a drag towards things that feel good now. I am myself shamed to say that in many ways I have been guilty of giving in to the world's system. But, that's not what the Lord wants for us! As teens, before adulthood crushes in, He wants us to learn to trust Him—not guys, money, or possessions. How we act now determines what future decisions we'll make. We must constantly "remember" God and turn our eyes on Him.

Reflection:

Are you taking advantage of ways to grow closer to God or turning to other things?

Application Step:

Seek out ways to daily remember God. Perhaps consider joining a Bible study, or even helping to begin a small group for girls in your church. Fellowship with other believers who earnestly seek God will grow your own faith. Pray for Him to shine a light in your heart where there may be sin that is making you feel distant from your Creator. Remember, Jesus gave His life for all our sin and those who seek Him will never be turned away.

Prayer:

Dear God, please forgive me for all the times I've turned from you to wish for worldly things like the best clothes or the attention of a guy. Help me to remember to ask you in every situation. Thank you for dying for me to be able to know and remember you. In Jesus name. Amen!

Weary

Are you weary?

Written by Heather Hart

Come to me, all you who are weary and burdened, and I will give you rest

~Matthew 11:28

Do you ever feel like the world is crashing down around you? Like, if one more thing goes wrong you will collapse under the weight of it all? I feel that way today. I was so stressed out, it just seemed like everything was going wrong. It really wasn't, but it sure did feel like it was. God kept reminding me that I was suppose to look to Him when I was weary, but with everything that was going on, it just seemed like I couldn't. Does that make since? Have you ever felt that way? Maybe you're failing a class and your parents are mad at you, or you're having a fight with your best friend. Maybe it seems like your life is all planned out for you and you don't feel like you can live up to expectations. Or maybe it's something different, but equally as weighty. It doesn't matter what it is, Jesus calls us to come to Him when we are weary and burdened.

We shouldn't wait until it feels like we have the time; we need to make the time. Just take a few moments to pray, or open the Bible and read His Word. As soon as I took that time today, as soon as I turned to Christ, I felt so much better. You see, when we take that time to come to Him, He gives us rest. He lifts the weight off of our shoulders, and reminds us that it really is in His hands and that we need to trust Him. That doesn't mean that everything will be downhill from there, it just reminds us that no matter how many bad things happen, He will never leave us or forsake us (Deuteronomy 31:8).

Reflection:

Do you feel weary or burdened? Are you trying to handle it all on your own, or are you going to Jesus to get rest from the world?

Application Step:

When you feel weary or burdened, like you just can't keep going, go to Jesus. Take a moment to pray, or step back from life for a moment and open your Bible. Remember that you are not alone, and that you don't have to carry the weight of the world, because it is all in God's reliable hands.

Prayer:

Lord, I need to be reminded of your provision. I just feel so weary sometimes. I don't feel like I can keep going, but when I come to you, oh Lord, you give me rest. You remind me that I don't have to face each day alone. You remind me that you will never leave me or forsake me, and that you are with me wherever I go. Thank you, Lord. Thank you for always being there and for giving me the rest I need to move forward with your help. In the name of your holy and precious Son I pray. Amen.

Ask

Have you prayed about that yet?
Written by Heather Hart

Listen to my cry for help, my King and my God, for to you I pray.
~Psalm 5:2

Do you ever complain about the simple things in life? I know I do. Sometimes I catch myself complaining about something that I know is just temporary. It might be an upset stomach, or I'm too hot or too cold, or maybe I'm hungry, the list goes on. I know these things don't last forever and I know they aren't going to kill me, yet I complain anyway.

Well, yesterday I was reading and it came to my attention that while I'm great at complaining, I don't always take the time to take my simple requests before God. I know that God cares about me, and that He cares about my circumstances, after all, He has every hair on my head numbered. I know that God has the power to meet my needs, or to meet me where I am and make me content, but so often I fail to ask.

It reminds me of the Israelites in the desert. They complained because they had no water, yet as soon as Moses took their request to the Lord, their need was met. All they had to do was ask. Of course there is the difference between needs and wants, but if we truly have a need, and we bring our request before God, we will not be forsaken (Joshua 1:5).

Reflection:

Are you complaining about something that you haven't even asked God to take care of yet?

Application Step:

Whenever you catch yourself complaining, remember that our God is powerful enough to meet your needs, and remember that He will not forsake you. Ask Him to take care of you, and then trust Him to make it so.

Prayer:

Lord God, I so often forget to ask you for things and go straight to complaining. Please forgive me. Help me to put my trust and my faith in you. Help me to remember that you are all powerful, and that you can take care of me, no matter what the circumstance. I love you, Lord. Thank you for loving me. In the name of your son, Jesus Christ, I pray. Amen.

Knocked Down

Only our King can put the pieces of our heart back together again.

Written by Heather Hart

He heals the brokenhearted and binds up their wounds.
                                                    ~Psalm 147:3

God is so amazing. I just love knowing that no matter where I am, He meets me there. When I am broken, He heals me. He binds up my wounds and helps me up off the ground. Do you ever need Him to do that for you? Maybe your heart is burdened with the loss of a loved one, or maybe you have had your heart broken by a boy. It could be that you have been wounded by someone in your family, or even one of your friends. Maybe you're teased at school, or flunking one of your classes. There are just so many things in this life that can leave us broken, so many things that can wound us and weigh us down. And that's why it's so encouraging to me to know that God is near (Jer. 23:23), and to know that He cares for me (1 Peter 5:7).

It reminds me of the story of humpty dumpty. You know, life knocked him down, and no one could put him back together again? Well, that's just it. When life knocks us down, God CAN put us back together again. He can meet us in our brokenness and restore us to something even more glorious than we were before we were shattered.

So, where ever you are today, no matter what kinds of hurts you are facing, I encourage you to look to our King. I encourage you to call on His name, and allow Him to meet you where you are, to pick you up, and bind your wounds because He cares for you.

Reflection:

Is your heart hurting today? Does it feel like you've been knocked down and are lying in pieces of the mess? Has something left you feeling broken?

Application Step:

Cry out to God. Ask Him to come into your heart, and to bring you healing. Then seek out someone else to pray with you, and encourage you through your time of healing (If you don't have anyone who can pray with you, simply e-mail us and we will join you in prayer-our contact information can be found in the back of this book).

Prayer:

Father God, I cry out to you right now. Lord, that you may hear me, and come to restore me, to make me whole again. I just feel so broken right now, Lord. I need you. I need the healing that can only be found in you. In the name of your holy Son I pray. Amen.

Chasing Dreams

What are you pursuing?

Written by Heather Hart

But you… pursue righteousness, godliness, faith, love, endurance and gentleness.

~1 Timothy 6:11

Today's world encourages us to chase after dreams of becoming rich, famous, and successful. It tells us that if we don't live up to its standards, that we have failed. But God measures our life by totally different standards. He tells us not to chase after those things, but instead to humble ourselves, give to those less fortunate, and not to measure our worth in worldly things (for the things of this world will pass away~ 1 John 2:17). If we spend our time chasing the dreams of this world, we will end up hurting for it, for the most successful person by the worlds standards will still die and all of his 'success' will be left on earth and no use to him. Worldly success can't save us. God knows that. That's why He sent His Son. Only Christ did what needed to be done to ensure that we aren't lost forever. Knowing this, we are encouraged to pursue spiritual things, not worldly things. In today's verse we are encouraged to seek after righteousness, godliness, faith, love, and gentleness. We are encouraged to endure this world, so that we can have hope of the things yet to come.

So instead of chasing after that guy at school that we've been eyeing, popularity, or the pair of shoes that we saw at the mall, we need to shift our focus. We need to start pursuing a closer relationship to Christ, love for His people, a right attitude, and the desire to do His will.

Reflection:

Have you been chasing after things of this world, or are you storing up your treasure in heaven?

Application Step:

"Do not store up for yourselves treasures on earth, where moth and rust destroy, and where thieves break in and steal. But store up for yourselves treasures in heaven, where moth and rust do not destroy, and where thieves do not break in and steal. For where your treasure is, there your heart will be also." ~ Matthew 6:19-21

Take a moment to re-evaluate your desires, goals, and actions. If needed, shift your focus and come up with new goals, commit to changing your actions and ask God for His help.

Prayer:

Father God, please help me to keep my eyes set on you. Help me to remember that the things of this world will pass away. No amount of popularity, money, clothing, or any person apart from Christ is capable of saving my soul. I love you, Lord. I really do. Help me to keep my focus on you, help me to reflect my love for you with my words, actions, and dreams. In the name of my Lord and Savior, Jesus Christ, I pray. Amen.

Devoted

Going through the motions
Written by Heather Hart

I remember the devotion of your youth, how as a bride you loved me and followed me through the wilderness, through a land not sown.

~Jeremiah 2:2

Do you remember when you first accepted Christ as your Savior? It doesn't have to be an exact moment, but just that time when you were so on fire for Him that you could hardly contain it? I do. It was an amazing feeling; I was totally and completely devoted to Him. However, as time went by, that fire started to dwindle. Yes, I still love Christ with all of my heart, but sometimes it feels like I am just going through the motions. Instead of reading my Bible out of devotion to God and the desire to know Him more, sometimes I just get into the habit of reading it because I know I'm supposed to. Instead of being devoted to my Bible reading, I'm simply reading devotions and checking them off my to-do list. Does that ever happen to you? Instead of doing something out of devotion to Christ, do you just do it because you have to? Maybe it's attending church or youth group, or singing worship songs? It might not even be because you have to, but just because it's fun. It doesn't matter why we are doing it, unless we are doing it out of devotion to Christ, then our motivation is wrong. Proverbs 16:2 says that all our ways seem innocent to us, but our motives are weighed by the Lord (paraphrased). God does care about our motives. He wants us to be devoted to Him, not just going through the motions.

Reflection:

Are you going through the motions, or are you totally devoted to Christ?

Application Step:

Evaluate your motivation for doing things. Do you go to church because you have to, because your friends are there, or because you want to spend time with Christ? What about singing and listening to Christian music, or reading your Bible?

Prayer:

Father God, help me to be devoted to you. I don't want to spend my life going through the motions. Instead, I want you to be my motivation. I want to desire you with all that I am. I want to be on fire for you, Lord. I want my heart to burn with a passion for you, a passion that motivates me to know you more. Help me in this. In Jesus' name. Amen.

Job

Praise through the pain

Written by Heather Hart

"...The LORD gave and the LORD has taken away; may the name of the LORD be praised."

~Job 1:21

I don't know about you, but sometimes I relate all too well to Job. I'm nowhere near the most upright person on earth, but sometimes it feels like the world is crashing down around me. Sometimes it just doesn't feel like it's worth it and I think it might be easier if I were never born. Have you ever felt that way?

In Job 3:25, Job said that he had no peace, quietness, or rest, only turmoil. Now, if Job, the most upright man on all the earth, can say that, then surely we aren't 'bad Christians' just because we feel that way too. Job went through a lot, but his story ended well. He lost everything he had and reached the point where he didn't feel like life was worth living, but he praised God through his pain, and in the end God blessed him beyond measure and gave him more than he had ever had before.

Like Job, we experience things in this world that are unpleasant to say the least. We experience sickness, death, pain, and just all kind of hardships, but Job's story gives me hope (and I hope it does the same for you). It's important to remember not to curse God, but to look to Him, to praise Him through our pain, even when we wish we didn't have to go on, because He will bring us through whatever we are going through. He will do it in His time, and in His way, but He will not abandon us. When all seems lost, Job's story assures me that God is there. He has a plan, and He will deliver us.

Reflection:

Can you relate to the way Job felt? No peace, joy, or rest, but only turmoil? Have you ever wished that you were never born?

Application Step:

I encourage you to praise God through your pain. Read through Job's story, and see what he went through and how God blessed him in the end.

Prayer:

Father God, sometimes I feel like Job. I feel like the world is just crashing down around me and like there is just no reason to go on. Lord, help me to remember that you are there during those times. You have promised to be close to the brokenhearted (Psalm 34:18). Thank you for always being there for me. Thank you for being such an awesome God, Lord! "I know that you can do all things, no plan of yours can be thwarted" (Job 42:2), Lord I just thank you for having my best interests at heart, please help me to remember praise you through my pain. In Christ's Name. Amen.

Quiet Time

Have you been listening?

Written by Heather Hart

The Sovereign LORD has given me an instructed tongue, to know the word that sustains the weary. He wakens me morning by morning, wakens my ear to listen like one being taught.

~Isaiah 50:4

I have been reading in the book of Isaiah lately and God has just been teaching me so much! Today's verse has quickly become my new favorite, because it holds such a great message. Here is my brief summary of that message:

> "To know the word that sustains the weary, we have to be in the Word. To be taught I have to listen, and I can't listen if I don't take the time."

As Christians we are taught to look to God for our strength. We know that He comforts the broken hearted, and just gives us everything we need each and every day. From grace to guidance, our God is suppose to be our go to guy! However, we can't know what He wants for us if we don't spend time with Him. He speaks to us through His Word, and if we aren't spending time reading His Word, we won't be able to hear Him. I know that I most often hear God's voice when something happens and a Scripture immediately comes to mind. That's God! He reminds me about what He has already said. But so many times I am left wondering what God wants for me, simply because I don't know His Word as well as I need too, and I haven't been spending time reading it like I should. The Word sustains the weary, and if I don't know it, and don't spend time learning it, it's going to be pretty hard for it to sustain me...

Knowing God's Word is only part of what's needed to hear His voice. The other part is being quiet before Him in prayer- to listen like one being taught. Just like we can't learn anything at school if we are talking instead of listening, it's almost impossible to hear God when we have our radios cranked up, or the TV blaring. When it's hard for us to concentrate long enough to finish a prayer, it's going to be even harder for us to hear His response. In today's world we live in a fast paced society that tells us that we should be able to get all the answers right now, but God doesn't work that way. He wants us to spend time WITH Him, and He will give us our answers when He is ready. As another verse in Isaiah reads: "As the heavens are higher than the earth, so are my ways higher than your ways and my thoughts than your thoughts." (55:9).

Reflection:

Have you been taking the time needed to know God's Word and hear His voice? Or are you simply too busy and drowning Him out with everything else that's going on in your life?

Application Step:

Spend some quiet time today with God. Turn off the TV, radio, your computer, and cell phone. Read His Word, and ask Him if there is anything He has been trying to tell you that you have been too busy to listen to.

Prayer:

Father God, forgive me for not taking the time to be with you. I long to hear your voice, but I often want it on my terms not yours. Forgive me for my selfish attitude towards you, for wanting everything in my time. Help me to spend more time with you. Help me to learn your word, and not to drown you out with everything going on in my life. In the name of your Son, Jesus Christ, I pray. Amen.

Perfect

Are you striving for perfection?
Written by Elissa Branum

*There is no fear in love. But **perfect** love drives out fear, because fear has to do with punishment.*
~1 John 4:18a

Have you ever felt afraid or unsure?

I'm almost sure that almost everyone one has. One major reason I feel afraid is actually because I fear failure. I feel like I'll never be "perfect."

We strive for perfection. It's like we are hard-wired to want the very best...yet we always fall short. Why is it so integrated in our psyche to admire and to desire perfection? Why do we envy those people who seem so "put together," like everything is great in their lives? Why do we point out the loveliest houses, cars, and other belongings?

Maybe we were meant to live **for** Someone capable of the perfection we fall short of. Maybe our hearts are tuned to the One who **is** perfect. Perhaps we are inwardly seeking and longing for His purest, closest, most right embrace. **Jesus** is the reason for our adoration of perfection.

Reflection:

Do you fear imperfection?

Application Step:

Maybe you, as I do, need to let go of your fear of falling short. Realize that God paid the price for our sins, and there is nothing we can do to earn that salvation. Talk to a godly adult if you are unsure, and fall into the arms of a perfect God.

Prayer:

Thank You, Lord, for being a perfect God. What more could we long for? Who else could fill us and take away our emptiness? I was made for you, Lord. Help me to believe that you are the only perfect One. I love you, Lord!

Forgetful

Where do your priorities lie?
Written by Heather Hart

Does a maiden forget her jewelry, a bride her wedding ornaments? Yet my people have forgotten me, days without number.

~Jeremiah 2:32

This verse just cuts me to the core. I never forget to get dressed in the morning, or to brush my hair, and I'm pretty sure that you don't either, but how often do we forget God? I can't even count the number of mornings where I have 'forgotten' (or even made a conscious choice not) to spend time with Him. We don't forget to go to school, but we might forget about the Bible study that we wanted to join, or lose track of time and end up running late to church or youth group.

When I read this verse, it really hit me that I have my priorities messed up. No, that doesn't mean that going to school isn't important, but how much MORE important should spending time with my Creator be? How can I call myself a Christian, and yet put more thought and effort into getting dressed then I do praying and reading my Bible?

Today, I am making the decision to answer the call that God gave to His people through His prophet Jeremiah (3:12-13):

"Return, faithless Israel... acknowledge your guilt- you have rebelled against the Lord your God, you have scattered your favors... and have not obeyed me."

Reflection:

Have you forgotten to make God your #1 priority?

Application Step:

Answer God's call and return to Him; make Him your #1 priority. For the next week, set aside a specific time each day to spend with God. Don't let life get in your way, but stick to it.

Prayer:

Father God, I admit that I have forgotten you. I have forgotten that I am nothing without you, that you are the very reason that I'm alive. Please forgive me for my unfaithfulness towards you, and thank you, God, for always being faithful to me, even when I turn my back on you. Help me to do better, Lord. Help me to remember you, and to spend time with you each and every day. Amen.

Obey

Obeying isn't always easy
Written by Heather Hart

Be very strong; be careful to obey... without turning to the right or to the left.
~Joshua 23:6

Do you always do what your parents say? Do you obey them no matter what they ask? Or do you sometimes think that you know better than them, or that what they are asking or demanding isn't important, or just plain mean? I remember one time when I was out with my friends, and my mom told me that I needed to come home when it got dark. When she told me, I didn't really care because that seemed so far away. However, it got dark a whole lot faster than I expected it too. I ended up convincing myself that I didn't need to go home, because the streetlights provided plenty of light. Let me tell you that my mom did NOT agree with that conclusion, and in the end I had to start coming home when the streetlights came on (and they come on way before it's actually dark out!).

I think sometimes we have the same attitude towards God and His Word. He is very specific about what is sin and what isn't, but we try to make gray areas. We say, oh this isn't REALLY sin because of yadda yadda yadda. But deep down I think that we really know what He meant, and what we are doing is wrong. Do you have anything like that going on in your life? God encourages us to be strong and careful to obey. He wants us to obey Him without turning to the right or to the left. In other words, He doesn't want us to make up excuses for why we take sinful paths when we know deep down that they are wrong.

Reflection:

Are you making excuses for disobeying God or your parents?

Application Step:

Whatever it is that you have been making excuses for to convince yourself that it isn't really wrong, confess it to God. Ask for His forgiveness, and decide to make the right decision regarding it from this day on.

Prayer:

Father God, I'm sorry. Obeying isn't always easy, and it doesn't always fit into my idea of the perfect day. Help me with that, Lord. I really do want to live a life that is pleasing to you. I want to follow your commands without straying from the course you have laid out for my life, but it's hard and I need your help. I can't do it without you, God. Thank you for promising to be there to help me through this, and for sending your Son to redeem me from my mistakes. In His name I pray. Amen.

Forgiveness

When bad things happen
Written by Heather Hart

But encourage one another daily, as long as it is called today, so that none of you may be hardened by sin's deceitfulness.

~Hebrews 3:13

Sometimes things happen to us that we don't understand. We are wronged, or hurt, by others. Maybe someone you love was murdered, or maybe you were abused or even raped. The only thing worse than the original pain, is going through that with no one to support you. We live in a fallen world with sinful people, and we don't always stop to think about other people. It's like the old phrase hurt people hurt people (coined by Sandra Wilson). Things that cause deep pain always hurt more than one person, and sometimes the person who is hurting the most suffers even more at the hands of those who should be there to comfort them.

Sadly I have been on both sides of this, and I'm sure that most everybody else in the world has experienced both sides of it as well. On the one side, I needed to learn to forgive not only the original wrong, but also my family or friends that caused even more pain. On the other side, I needed to seek forgiveness from my friend that I ended up hurting by not looking past my own pain enough to see that I was hurting them more. Forgiveness isn't always easy, especially when we are hurting, but I tell you what, I felt a lot better after embracing forgiveness, and I bet you will too.

Reflection:

Do you need to forgive someone who has made a painful situation worse for you, or seek forgiveness from someone that you might have hurt because you were in pain?

Application Step:

Ask God to help you through the forgiveness process, and then go and embrace forgiveness.

Prayer:

Father God, help me to forgive those who hurt me both intentionally, and unintentionally. And, Lord, I pray that you help me to remember that I'm not the only one who is hurting. Help me to give grace to those who are hurting with me, and to be careful not to cause them more pain. I need your help to extend forgiveness to those who have done me wrong, but also to seek forgiveness from those whom I have hurt without thinking. Help me not to be selfish in my pain, Lord. Amen.

Spiritual Clothing

What are you wearing?
Written by Heather Hart

Therefore, as God's chosen people, holy and dearly loved, clothe yourselves with compassion, kindness, humility, gentleness and patience.

~Colossians 3:12

God tells us that we should be clothing ourselves with spiritual clothing. He doesn't care so much about the outside, it's what's on the inside that He is concerned about. Yet I find that so often when I get dressed in the morning, I only get dressed on the outside. I forget to get dressed spiritually. The result isn't so pretty. I tend to be moody, self-centered, and well, just plain unpleasant to be around! That's the exact opposite of how God wants His people to behave, however it is the normal sinful nature of humans, and after all, I am human.

Lately I have been noticing that just as each morning I have to put a conscious effort into putting on my clothes, it takes a conscious effort to have the attitude that God wants from His people. In other words, I have to make the conscious decision to put on my spiritual clothing. My attitude is a choice that I make. I can choose to be self-centered, self-righteous, judgmental, and well, you get the point, or I can choose to show kindness, compassion, humility, gentleness, and patience. But I have to make the choice. I have to take the time to evaluate each situation, and look to God to see how He would want me to react. I have to choose whether I want to walk around in my naked sinful human nature, or if I want to put on my spiritual clothing each day. What about you, did you remember to get dressed today?

Reflection:

Are you walking around in your naked sinful human nature, or are you taking the time to clothe yourself spiritually with kindness, humility, compassion, gentleness, and patience?

Application Step:

Make yourself a note to put on your spiritual clothing. It could be as simple as writing down today's verse and taping it to the bathroom mirror, next to your bed, or in your locker at school. Then make a conscious effort to wear your spiritual clothing each day.

Prayer:

Father God, I know that I am a human and that it's in my nature to sin, but Lord, I don't want to! Help me to remember to clothe myself with compassion, kindness, humility, gentleness, and patience each day, all day. Help me to remember that not everything is about me and that other people have feelings too, and then lead me to respond to them in a way that honors you. Help me to be more like Jesus, who you sent to live a life on earth to show us the way to live. It is in His name that I pray. Amen.

In His Name

But I want it now!!!!
Written by Heather Hart

You may ask me for anything in my name, and I will do it.
~John 14:14

Have you ever wanted something so bad, but never got it? I remember when I was little, I prayed and prayed that God would magically heal my prosthetic eye and make it real (kind of like the fairy in Pinocchio made him a real boy). All I wanted was to be normal, just like everyone else. I prayed, and prayed, and prayed, but it never happened. I would look at this verse in John, and get angry at God. He promised! I would say. It was a long hard road to learning the true meaning of this verse.

Over the years I have learned that asking for something in the name of Jesus, isn't simply tacking His name onto the end of my prayers. It isn't a guarantee that I will get everything I could ever dream of while I live on this earth, it's learning to ask for things that will bring glory to Christ. It's remembering James 4:3 that says when we ask and do not receive it's because we are asking with the wrong motives. It's asking for something that isn't motivated by my own selfishness. You see, I don't need to have two real eyes to glorify God. Having two normal eyes would be nice, but in the grand scheme of things, it wouldn't change who I am, who God is, or really anything other than my ability to watch 3D movies. There are so many more important things that I could spend my time praying about.

What about you? Have you ever asked God for something and gotten upset when He didn't make your wish His command? It could be something like a date with the guy in your math class, or that your pimple would go away. It might be asking Him to restore your parent's marriage, or to bring your friend back to life. There are millions of things that I remember asking God for that His answer wasn't yes to. In the end, I'm glad He told me know on some of them. He really does know best.

Reflection:

Are you upset that God hasn't given you the desires of your heart?

Application Step:

Check your motives. Then, pray and ask God for His will to be done and not your own. Ask Him to help you get through the struggle that you might be going through with His help, and to look to Him to carry you through and not a change in circumstances.

Prayer:

Father God, I sometimes get carried away with my selfish desires. I think I know what's best for me or those around me, and I get upset when things don't go my way. Help me to remember that you have my best interest at heart, even when I can't see it. Help me to trust you with the lives of my friends and family, Lord. Help me to ask for things with pure motives. In the name of your Son, Jesus Christ, I pray. Amen.

Mary's Song

What is your soul magnifying?

Written by Heather Hart

And Mary said "My soul glorifies the Lord and my spirit rejoices in God my Savior
~Luke 1:46 & 47

One of my favorite Christmas CD's to listen to is "Glory in the Highest: Christmas Songs of Worship" by Chris Tomlin. As I was listening to it one morning, the song "My Soul Magnifies the Lord" came on, and I couldn't help but think about Mary. The title of this song comes from Luke 1:46 (KJV) where Mary is singing of her love for God, and about how blessed she is for being chosen to carry the Savior of the world.

I don't know if you have ever taken the time to study the Christmas story, but very few people during the time it was actually going on thought Mary was blessed. In fact, she and Joseph weren't treated well at all. Even Joseph almost abandoned her during this time. She was an unmarried, pregnant teenager. You might be able to imagine how she was treated. Yet here she is, singing praises to God, and rejoicing in Him. That speaks a lot about her perspective on life. It would have been easy to curl up and cry. To let all of the harsh words get her down, but she chose to praise God for what He was doing in her life.

I don't know where you are at today. You might be that pregnant teenager, or you might have a million other things that seem to be going wrong in your life, but I encourage you, no matter where you are, to read Mary's song today. Take some time and just soak in her words. No matter where you are, God sees you. He knows where you are, and He is doing great things for you, even when you can't see it.

Reflection:

Are you letting the people of this world bring you down, or are you praising God even when life is hard?

Application Step:

Read Luke 1:46-55 and think about all the ways that you can use that same song to praise God in your life. Think of the great things that He has done for you, and praise Him for his provision, mercy, and tender loving care.

Prayer:

Father God, thank you; thank you so much for everything that you have done for me. I don't always feel like singing praises to you, but I am simply inspired by Mary's song. Help me to have that attitude of gratitude that she so clearly showed through her praise. Life isn't always easy, and there are defiantly some things that are harder to go through than others. I just ask you, Lord, that you will help me to remember that you are always with me, and doing great things, even when I can't see it. Help me to glorify you, no matter what I'm going through. Amen.

Why?

A Question We Often Ask When Bad Things Happen...
Written by Shelley Hitz

Trust in the Lord with all your heart and lean not on your own understanding;

~Proverbs 3:5

As we travel across the United States, we pray for divine appointments. What I mean by a divine appointment is an encounter with another person that God puts in our path - someone who either encourages us, or that we encourage in some way spiritually.

Recently, as we were traveling, we stayed in an RV park. And as we were getting ready to leave, I took a shower in their public showers. I finished drying my hair and getting dressed, and I was just about ready to leave when Teri walked in. We started talking and one thing led to another and before I knew it, she was telling me her life story.

I asked her if I could pray for her right there and she agreed and let me pray for her. As we talked more, I found out that Teri had layer upon layer of hurt and heartache in her life – wounds that were deep; issues that I will never understand. She had been sexually abused by her father as a young child. Not only that, her mother, who was addicted to prescription medications and drugs, gave her to her father to have sex with him. As she would cry afterward because of the pain and while her mother was cleaning her up, her mom would say hurtful things to her. These things left deep scars and deep wounds in her.

The amazing thing is that Teri wasn't even supposed to be there at the showers that time that day. She was actually going to go to the bank and had several errands to run, but felt like God told her to come to the RV park. I told her I believed it was a divine appointment.

We talked about forgiveness and how I will never understand this side of heaven why certain things happen. One of those things that I won't understand fully is why this type of abuse happened to her and many others around the world.

One day as I was struggling to understand the answers to some "why" questions in my own life, God gave me a powerful illustration. He showed me that for me to try to understand "why" and figure out my life is like teaching a two year old physics and calculus. No matter how much you try to explain these subjects to a two year old, they will not understand it. Their brains are not developed to the point to fully comprehend these topics.

I believe in the same way, God has shown me that I'm like that two year old trying to understand why bad things happen to people in this world. There are certain things that I believe I will not fully understand until I get to heaven. Why? Well, because I still have a human brain. I am not God. So, on that day, as Teri and I talked about how important forgiveness is - even though she has every excuse and every right in the world to not want to forgive her mother for what had happened - that forgiveness is truly what will set her free and allow her to begin healing from the inside out.

We prayed together again. After we finished praying, Teri hugged me and I saw hope in her eyes. Even though I don't have all the answers, I do know the One who does. He reminds me to bring my concerns, my questions, and the things I don't understand to Him. He is able to carry them. Many times He does give us understanding and clarity this side of heaven, but when He doesn't, like the quote from Proverbs that I shared in the beginning of this devotion, I want to trust in the Lord with all my heart, and lean not on my own understanding.

Reflection:

Are you trusting God with all your heart, or are you trying to figure out all of the answers on your own?

Application Step:

Take some time right now to pray and ask God to help you to trust in Him. Give whatever has been bugging you lately to Him, and trust Him to deal with it.

Prayer:

Father God, I so often lean on my own understanding. I can't explain it, Lord, but for some reason it just seems like I need to. But I don't. Help me to put all of my trust in you. Help me to trust you with EVERYTHING, not just the easy stuff.

Restore my hope, Lord. In the name of your Son I pray. Amen.

Scars

...and the story left behind
Written by Heather Hart

See, I have engraved you on the palms of my hands;
~Isaiah 49:16

Things in this life leave scars. Some scars are physical, while others are emotional. Both were left behind by something painful, however the scar is only part of what is left. Have you ever sat around with someone talking about your scars? I have done this on a few occasions. I have a scar on my arm from when a friend was trying to scare me and pretend to run me over with his bike, only I realized what was going on and tried to jump out of the way at the same time he gave up on me jumping out of the way and turned. We both went the same direction and he did run me over. I had a huge cut on my arm, and his handlebars were all bent up (I declare myself the winner of that battle). I have a really cool scar on my finger that's shaped like a Nike sign, but I don't remember where it came from... Then there are, of course, the emotional scars left behind from life.

However, my favorite scars to ponder on aren't my own. I have a friend who has scars on His hands. One in each where they were pierced with nails. You see, these are my favorite scars because He got them saving me from eternal hell. He loved me so much that He gave His life so that I could live. But not just for me, He did it for you too. When I look at my scars, I see memories made, or memories lost, but I also remember His scars. I remember what He did for me, and for you. No matter what the story behind my scars is, or even the story behind yours, He got His scars to save us from ours. Only He could heal the scar left behind by the sexual abuse of my step father. Only His scars were created to cover both the scar that left in me, and the sin of the person that caused it. And you know what? His scars can heal your wounds, and cover over your sin as well. Whether you have been scarred or caused scars, He's got you covered. All you have to do is trust and believe.

Reflection:

Do you have physical or emotional scars surrounded by stories of hurt?

Application Step:

Take some time to look at your scars (physical or emotional), then remember that Jesus came to live and to die so that those scars didn't have to cause you pain. When you look at your scars, remember that He has scars too, and His scars are there for you.

Prayer:

Father God, Thank you. Thank you so much for sending Jesus to this world to live and to die for me. Thank you for reminding me that His scars are there for me. He did everything for me, Lord. I am so amazed by that. Help me to remember His scars when I look at my own. In His glorious name I pray. Amen.

Commissioned

Eager to Serve
Written by Heather Hart

"Here am I. Send me!"

~Isaiah 6:8

As I was reading in Isaiah today, this verse just resonated within me. "Here I am. Send me!" Isaiah begs. I must admit, I don't use those words very often. I can relate so well to the rest of Isaiah's words, but I don't often ask God to send me places. Earlier in this chapter Isaiah is realizing how unworthy he is next to our righteous God. I can totally relate to that. If my standard is Christ, I fall incredibly short. God knows that, that's why He sent Christ. But while Christ was on earth, He called us to go. He issued what is known as the great commission. He told His followers to go into all of the world and to teach all nations about Him. Essentially He commanded us to echo Isaiah's words.

We don't have to ask to be sent, we have been told to go. But how often do we? So often we worry more about what the world thinks of us instead of what God has called us to do. We worry that we will get funny looks, instead of realizing that without the truth of Christ the person we are afraid to speak about Christ to will spend eternity in hell. Isaiah wasn't worried about that. He was eager to serve. When he asked God how long he should spend telling people about Him, the answer was forever. Not a simple, oh just mention it once and then leave people alone. But tell them, keep telling them, don't ever stop proclaiming the Truth until the world has come to an end. And Isaiah was eager to obey. He didn't care that he would be considered a weirdo, his only desire was to serve our awesome God. Where does that leave us? Where does that leave me when I'm too nervous to go over and tell the girl in the corner that Jesus loves her and invite her to church?

Reflection:

Are you eager to serve by following the call of the great commission?

Application Step:

Ask for God to give you the strength to speak out for Him, and ask Him to show you someone specific to talk to about Him. When you get the answer to that prayer, follow through.

Prayer:

Father, I am so selfish. Please forgive me for worrying more about myself then the souls of others. Give me the strength now, and in the future to speak up for your glory. Help me to tell others about you, Lord. Give me the eagerness that Isaiah had to serve you. I want to tell people about what your Son has done for us. I just need your help to find the strength to speak up for Him. It is in His name that I pray. Amen.

A Lesson from Haiti

Life isn't easy
Written by Shelley Hitz

The thief comes only to steal and kill and destroy; I have come that they may have life, and have it to the full.

~John 10:10

Becoming a Christian isn't a free ticket to a perfect of easy life. It doesn't even mean that life will be better than it was before. Actually, Jesus promised us that in this world we will have troubles (John 16:33). One of the times that God has shown me the truth of that statement was on January 12th, 2010, when an earthquake shook the nation of Haiti. Many lives were devastated by the earthquake that day, and I had the opportunity to go to Haiti as part of a medical relief team, merely four weeks after the earthquake hit. What I saw in Port-au-Prince, Haiti, rocked my world! I had never experienced anything like it before.

I have traveled to several third world countries before. I have been to Africa and to Ecuador. I have lived in the country of Belize and ministered in Guatemala for two years. So, I know what it is like to travel to a third world country and I know what it is like to see poverty. Not only did Haiti have the poverty, but after the earthquake there was also so much trauma. People lost their homes, their jobs, their lives, their limbs. There was so much tragedy and heartache.

When something like this happens, many times people try to explain why. However, God has shown me a verse in the Bible that has given me some insight on the topic of "why bad things happen." That verse is John 10:10. It says, "The thief comes to steal, kill and destroy." The thief is referring to Satan, the devil, or Lucifer, however you want to call him. The verse, though, goes on to say, "But I, Jesus, have come to give life and life to the full".

From this verse, God has shown me that Satan is the author of anything that steals, kills or destroys. So, if we have had something stolen from us, if something is killed within us or destroyed, who is the author of that? It is not God. It comes from Satan…because he is the one that steals, kills and destroys.

We live in a fallen world. John 16:33 says, "In this world, you will have troubles." It doesn't say might; it doesn't say maybe; it doesn't say if you're a good Christian or if you have enough faith that you won't have troubles. It says you will have trouble. But then it goes on to say, "But take heart, I, Jesus, have overcome this world."

As a believer in Jesus, when we have a relationship with Him, we have hope…even in the midst of hardship and difficult times. I witnessed that in Haiti. I witnessed people who had a relationship with Jesus and in the midst of their pain, in the midst of their destruction, having witnessed death all around them they had hope. In the small hospital where I worked our patients would sing praises and worship God each night.

One night they brought all of the workers out into the main hospital area and blessed us. They wanted to bless us with a prayer. They prayed and blessed us in such an amazing way. I have never been prayed for like that before. And even though I couldn't fully understand what they were saying because they were speaking in Haitian Creole, I kept hearing them say thank you, thank you. As I stood there watching the patients I had come to help - blessing me and thanking God for me - in the midst of their pain, tears streamed down my face. They were tears of joy in the midst of sorrow.

Reflection:

Are you letting Satan steal, kill, and destroy your life and your joy, or are you focusing on the hope that is found in Christ?

Application Step:

Instead of focusing on the bad things that are going on, cling to God's promise that He will deliver you. Cling to the fact that Jesus came to give us life to the full, and trust in Him to come through for you. Shift your focus to the things that you can praise Him for, and then do just that.

Prayer:

Father God, I don't always understand why bad things happen, but I do know that you have promised to always be there for me. Thank you for that promise. Thank you for the hope that I have in Christ. I ask you now Lord, just to show me things to praise you for. Help me to focus on the things that you are doing for good, not on all the things that don't seem to be going my way. In the name of your Son I pray. Amen.

Self-Image

The pearls of God
Written by Heather Hart

So God created man in his own image, in the image of God he created him; male and female he created them.
~Genesis 1:27

This is one of those verses that seems to just keep popping up everywhere I turn. And every time I have heard someone say it, they have been referring to our self-esteem and the self-image we have of ourselves as humans. I guess that for me at least, it's easiest to remember that God made mankind out of the dust of the ground. That seems to be more relatable then pondering on being made in His image for me. I think as humans, we tend to beat ourselves up too much, and I'm sure Satan just has a hay day when we are too busy beating ourselves up to be of any use to Christ. Satan enjoys it when we look at ourselves and all we see is a pile of dirt. But that isn't what God sees. God created us in HIS own image. We were created in the image of God! How awesome is that?! So why is it that we can't see past the materials used in creation to the final product?

While there are lots of things where the material is far less than the final product (well, in just about every situation that holds to be true), I love the picture painted by a pearl, because it starts out just as we did. While God made us from the dust of the ground, pearls are made from a single grain of sand. It takes time for the oysters to mold the sand into the finished gem, just as it takes time for God to smooth out our rough edges. So while we may be tempted to look at ourselves and see a useless pile of dirt, God looks at us and sees His beautiful pearls.

Reflection:

Do you see yourself as a pile of dirt, or a beautiful pearl made in the image of God?

Application Step:

I encourage you to look past the materials God used to create mankind, and focus on the fact that you were created in His image. Get out your journal, or just a random notebook, and write about who God is, and how your image reflects that (a good starting point would be that God is valuable, and so are you – Mathew 18:12-14).

Prayer:

Father God, help me to remember that I was made in your image. That's something that isn't really very easy for me to grasp. It's so easy to listen to the insults of others, and then to use them to make myself feel even worse about myself. But your Word tells me that I was made in your image. You are not a pile of dirt, Lord. You are an awesome God. You are smart, talented, and just plain wonderful. Whenever I'm tempted to beat myself up, please remind me of the qualities that I have in common with you. Help me to remember that I am your pearl in the making, and remind me to be patient while you smooth out my rough edges.

Attitude

Resentment, grudges and forgiveness
Written by Heather Hart

And the Lord's servant must not quarrel; instead, he must be kind to everyone, able to teach, not resentful.
~2 Timothy 2:24

Not resentful... If you're anything like me, I imagine that those words sting just a little. When people sin against us, it's hard not to resent them. I mean, that girl that slept with my boyfriend, do you have any idea how hard it was for me to forgive her? It definitely wasn't easy! It seems like it's always easier to hold a grudge then it is to forgive and move on. Have you ever experienced anything like that?

There are lots of things that can cause us to resent others: rumors, harsh words, or actions taken against us. I remember one time when the student teacher gave me a detention because the teacher's pet stole my test and when I reached to get it back from her, she screamed and said that I hit her. I didn't. He knew I didn't, but he punished me anyway because she was his favorite. He later apologized, but it was still hard to move past the mark on my record for something that I didn't do. It was really hard for me to learn to be kind to him, and to her for that matter, after that experience. But today's verse reminds me that no matter what others do to us, we need to forgive them, not resent them. We have to show kindness, no matter what kind of attitude they have towards us. It's not easy, but it's what God wants.

I don't know what situations you have been in that caused you to become resentful. It could have been a teacher giving you an unfair grade (or detention), or it could be an action taken by a friend. In the end though, God says it doesn't matter. He says that if we are His servants (Christians), then we must be kind to EVERYONE, and not resentful.

Reflection:

Is there anyone that you have been holding a grudge against?

Application Step:

Forgive! Ask God to help you honor Him by being kind towards everyone, and letting go of all of the resentment you have been holding onto.

Prayer:

Father God, I admit that it's hard for me not to resent some of the actions taken by others. Their words and actions hurt me, God. I need your help to learn to forgive them and let it go. I need your help to be kind to them, even when they have caused me pain. In the name of your Son, who came so that all could be forgiven, I pray. Amen.

Hope

Confidently expecting something yet to come

Written by Heather Hart

For in this hope we were saved. But hope that is seen is no hope at all. Who hopes for what he already has? But if we hope for what we do not yet have, we wait for it patiently.
~Romans 8:24-25

Hope is something that the Bible talks about often. Today's verse tells us that it is by hope that we are saved. It only makes since to me to take a moment to make sure that my hope is in the right thing. The verses before the ones above tell us that all creation hopes for redemption, and in Colossians 1:27 and 1 Timothy 1:1, we are assured that our hope is Christ.

The hope that Christians have is that Christ really did live, die, and rise again, but our hope doesn't end there. Our hope is that He will return, and because we have believed in Him, that we will spend eternity with Him. Now that is something worth hoping for, but is that truly where we put our hope?

It seems so easy to place our hope in other things, things that seem to be more obtainable. We hope that we are good enough, we hope that we go to the right church, or even that God doesn't really care and everyone goes to heaven. However, none of those things will have the outcome that we hope for. Our hope is only founded in Christ.

Reflection:

What do you hope for? Is your hope in the things of this world, or is it firmly planted in our Savior?

Application Step:

Take some time today to think about the hope that we have in Christ. Ask God to help you put your hope in Him, and keep your eyes on the prize.

Prayer:

Heavenly Father, the promise that you have given us in Christ is truly amazing. The hope that we have because of it will never cease to amaze me. Help me to live in that hope. Help me to put my hope in Christ's work on the cross and in my life, as well as in His promised return. Help me to keep that as my focus, Lord. In the name of Hope, I pray. Amen.

Black and White

Did God really say that?
Written by Heather Hart

Now the serpent was more crafty than any of the wild animals the LORD God had made. He said to the woman, "Did God really say, 'You must not eat from any tree in the garden'?"
~Genesis 3:1

Most of us have heard the story of the fall too many times to count. But when I was reading through it today, I couldn't help but think about Paul's words in Philippians 4 verse 8: *...whatever is true, whatever is noble, whatever is right, whatever is pure, whatever is lovely, whatever is admirable—if anything is excellent or praiseworthy—think about such things.* The serpent used one of what is probably his favorite tactics when he began his dialog with Eve. If I had to hazard a guess, this is still probably the same tactic he uses each and every day to encourage us to sin. He simply shifted Eve's attention away from the things that are right, and onto the possibility of sin.

Can you see that in your life? Do you ever think, "Did God really say this? Is this really in God's Word?" and then let your mind wonder to the consequences of disobedience, rather than focusing on all of the wonderful things that God has given you? I'm guilty of that. It's so easy for my mind to wander. To think about things that aren't pure. Did God really say that I couldn't tell my friends what so and so did yesterday? Does that really count as gossip? No, it's just venting, and venting is healthy right? - Wrong! We are supposed to think about the things that are praiseworthy, not gossip worthy. Okay... but what about this, or that. It's so easy to let my mind wonder to what is technically sin. Do you ever have that happen? Instead of focusing on what God did say, and what we know to be true, we let our minds wander to the things that aren't black and white.

I encourage you today to ignore the crafty serpent, and focus on Paul's words instead: *...whatever is true, whatever is noble, whatever is right, whatever is pure, whatever is lovely, whatever is admirable—if anything is excellent or praiseworthy—think about such things.* (Phi. 4:8)

Reflection:

Do you let your mind wander to things that are grey areas, or do you keep your mind focused on thoughts that you know are praiseworthy?

Application Step:

Write down Philippians 4:8 somewhere where you will see it often. Post it in your locker, or on the mirror in your bedroom. Tape it inside your binder, just somewhere where it will confront you time after time. Today, keep your thoughts focused on thoughts that you know are praiseworthy. If it isn't something you would want to tell your parents or your pastor, then it probably isn't something you should be thinking about.

Prayer:

Father God, help me to keep my mind focused on you. Help me to think about things that are true, noble, right, and praiseworthy. Don't let me fall into the trap of the crafty serpent, Lord. Help me to remember what you have said through your servant Paul. Help me to take every thought captive and make it obedient to Christ (2 Cor. 10:5). It is in His name that I pray; to Him be the glory. Amen.

Passions

Express yourself
Written by Heather Hart

There are different kinds of gifts, but the same Spirit. There are different kinds of service, but the same Lord. There are different kinds of working, but the same God works all of them in all men.

~1 Corinthians 12:4-6

I just love the fact that God gave each and every one of us unique personalities. Some of us are movie buffs, others get more into books, video games, or sports - and that's okay. That is how God created us. He created us with passions, talents and interests. He created us for different things, and with different passions. That came to my mind today while I was reading an article a friend shared on their blog. It was about how we are all passionate about different things, how we get excited about different events, books, or whatever, but the one thing that should remain the same, is our passion for our Savior. You see, even though we were all created uniquely for the glory of God, and God gave us all our own personalities and interests, we were still all created for the glory of God. We serve Him in different ways, but as Christians, we should still have a desire for Him, and for serving Him.

I guess that the point is that while God created us to be passionate people, there is an issue if that passion stops when we come before our creator. When we get totally psyched about the new outfit we just got or the new chick flick that is coming out, but we drag our feet when we have to get up early in the morning for church. When we can't wait to read our new book, or play that new video game, but we don't have the energy left to read God's Word.

God created passionate people. He sent Jesus so that we could live life to the full (John 10:10)! God wants us to be the people that He created us to be - to express ourselves. But as Jesus took the time to remind us, out of the overflow of the heart, the mouth speaks (Luke 6:45). Our passions reflect what is in our hearts. If we aren't as passionate about our Savior as we are about our shoes, we might need to take some time to reevaluate our hearts…

Reflection:

Are you more passionate about worldly things, or about the Creator of the world?

Application Step:

Spend sometime today thinking about our awesome God. Remember that He is the creator of the world. Without Him, your favorite pastime wouldn't even exist. Thank Him for the opportunity to express yourself, and for all of the wonderful things He has brought into your life.

Prayer:

Father God, I love you so much! Please help me to express the love that I have for you, just as much, no, more than the love that I have for the things you have created. Help me to show others that you truly are more important than my boyfriend, my favorite shoes, and everything else in my life, Lord. Help me to honor you, God. Thank you for allowing me to express myself, but help me to do so in a way that is pleasing to you. I want you to be the overflow of my heart. I want to be more passionate for you, than for anything else. Thank you for everything you do for me - especially for sending your Son, Jesus Christ, to die for my sins. It is in His name that I pray today. Amen.

The Price

Paid in full

Written by Heather Hart

But he was pierced for our transgressions, He was crushed for our iniquities; the punishment that brought us peace was upon Him, and by His wounds we are healed.

~Isaiah 53:5

Have you ever done something that made your parents mad? Okay, we probably all have gotten into trouble at one time or another, but I mean REALLY mad. Take a moment and just think about the most trouble that you have ever been in. Got it? Good, now can you imagine having your best friend coming over to your house and serving out that punishment for you? Would you casually toss a "thanks!" over your shoulder as you ran out the door to go to the movies with some of your other friends? Would you then not even speak to them the next day at school because you were too busy for them? Probably not, but yet that's how we treat Christ. That is what God did for us, only on a much grander scale. He sent His one and only Son to pay the price for our sin, and yet we treat it as just another fact of life. We committed the crime, and He did the time.

The words in today's verse tell us that the punishment He took for us, brought us peace; the peace of knowing that we don't have to spend eternity in hell for our sins. We deserve to, but we don't have to because God so loved the world that He sent

His Son to die for us (John 3:16). Jesus was crushed for our iniquities, and pierced for our transgressions; He paid our penalty in full. He said from the cross that it was finished. We no longer have to pay for our sins, because He took the punishment... all of it. Surely we owe Him more than we can ever repay, and certainly more than an hour on Sunday mornings.

Reflection:

Have you been taking Jesus, and the blood He paid for your sins for granted?

Application Step:

Get out your journal or just a piece of paper and write this verse down. Then write down some thoughts that go along with it. What does this mean in your life? What sins have you committed that are covered by His blood? What peace do you have now, that you wouldn't have if Jesus hadn't died that day 2,000 years ago as the punishment for your sins?

Prayer:

Father God, I am so sorry. I live my life without hardly even thinking of the sacrifice that Christ made on my behalf. It's so easy to go on with life and forget about the punishment that I don't have to serve because of Him. Help me to remember, Lord. Help me to remember what He has done for me, what you have done, God. Help me to live my life knowing that Christ took the punishment that I deserved, He took it all. I don't want to continue to blow Him off. Help me to honor Him with my words and actions, because even if I can never repay the price of my sins, I want Him to know how much He means to me.

Prayer & Praise

It's all about me
Written by Heather Hart

Is any one of you in trouble? He should pray. Is anyone happy? Let him sing songs of praise.

~James 5:13

I don't know about you, but in my life, when things aren't going my way, I tend to get upset; I worry. And when things are going my way, I get excited. I think about all of the things that I am doing right. Either way, it's all about me, me, me. I think that as humans, this is our default setting. After all, we live in our bodies and we never get a break from living our life. From our sinful human perspectives, it's easy to see life as all about us. The "It's All About Me" slogan is known all over America, and is displayed on bill boards, in stores, on shirts, posters, and even socks. That's exactly what Satan wants us to believe. That life is all about us. But God has called us for something greater. He wants us to realize that it isn't all about us. When things go wrong, He doesn't want us to worry when we are in trouble, but instead, He wants us to cast our cares upon Him (1 Peter 5:7). And when life is going great, He doesn't want us to be wrapped up in how awesome we think we are, He wants us to praise Him. Because it isn't all about us, it's about what Christ has done. I, for one, know that I need to remember that more often, instead of getting caught up in the world of me.

Reflection:

Are you focused on your joy or your pain, or are you praying and praising your God and King?

Application Step:

Take some time right now to pray. Bring your cares to Him, and entrust them to His care. Then, turn on some worship music and praise Him!

Prayer:

Father God, thank you for being you. You are so amazing, Lord. You are capable of handling the problems of the entire world that you created. You do mighty works every day. All I have is because of you, and I am so thankful for you. Please help me to trust you when things don't seem to be going my way. Help me to remember that you know what's best, and that you will work everything out for the good of those who love you (Rom. 8:28). In the name of your holy and precious Son I pray. Amen.

Anger

Good intentions with bad vibrations
Written by Heather Hart

You intended to harm me, but God intended it for good to accomplish what is now being done...
~Genesis 50:20

I finished reading the book of Genesis last night, and the words of Joseph just resounded in my head today. You see, my cat knocked over a vase and it soaked all of the papers on my desk, my keyboard, and even my computer. As I sat staring at the mess before me, I had to force myself to look beyond this world. I felt like I had a right to be angry, just like Joseph did. I lost so much work, and it took so long to clean up the mess. Yeah, it could have been worse, but still I felt justified in my anger. Likewise, Joseph had ever right to hate his brothers for what they did to him, I think we would all agree that he had the 'right' to be angry, but he let it go.

It's times like these when I have to force myself to take my focus off of myself, and everything that just happened, and put it onto Christ. I have to acknowledge that the things of this world really aren't as important as they seem. Yes my computer is expensive, but it wasn't ruined. Yes, I worked hard on all of my notes that are no longer legible, but if the thoughts were from God, then they will come again. If not, it's better to have them gone. I guess that it's important to remember that God is more important than whatever I am fuming about. Taking the focus off of myself and my situation and praising God and what He has done for us always helps me put things into perspective.

I don't know what kind of things make your blood boil, you might have every right in the world to be angry, but God doesn't want us to live that way. He wants us to live life to the full, and that means letting go of our anger and looking to see what God is trying to accomplish through our situation. So as I sort through my papers to decide what I can keep and what is totally trashed, I keep remembering the words of Joseph, "God intended it for good." I don't know how this is good, and I may not ever understand, but I have to trust that God is good, and let go of my anger as we are commanded to do at the end of Ephesians 4.

Reflection:

Are you focusing on things of this world, or on what God has planned? Are you staying angry, or are you letting go and moving on?

Application Step:

Take a moment right now to read Ephesians 4:29-32.
Whenever you are tempted by anger, remember that God might be intending the situation for good, even if you can't see how.

Prayer:

Father God, please forgive me for being angry. It's so hard to let go when things go so wrong. Help me to remember the words of Joseph when I start to get mad. Help me remember that even if the situation looks bad, that you can still use it for good. And then, Lord, help me to remember the words in Ephesians and get rid of all the anger, bitterness, and just any thoughts, behaviors or moods that do not benefit others or bring glory to you. Thank you for all that you do for me. In the name of your Son, Jesus Christ, I pray. Amen.

Surrender

Saved by grace
Written by Heather Hart

Those who cling to worthless idols forfeit the grace that could be theirs.

~Jonah 2:8

The grace of God truly is an amazing thing. The book of Ephesians tells us that it is by grace that we are saved, and that grace doesn't come from ourselves, but is a gift from God (2:8). I tend to forget that too often. Well, I guess to forget it at all would be too often, but I forget it more than I would like to admit. You see, gifts aren't something that we can earn. We have no choice in when we receive them or what they look like. We just have to accept them. It's a hard thing to feel like you have no control. It's so much easier to do something then nothing. But when it comes to our salvation, that's exactly what we are expected to do, nothing. We can't earn our way to heaven. We can't earn the grace of God. We simply have to accept it.

I was looking online for a different verse tonight when I stumbled across Jonah 2:8. It really made me stop for a second and just think about the difference between idols and grace. Idols are anything that we put before God. So if I'm trying to earn God's grace, then I am really forfeiting it by making myself and my abilities and idol to me. God has already told me that He is capable, but I have to surrender my will, and let

Him be my everything. To receive His grace, I have to do nothing! Now, if you're anything like me, you know that that's a lot harder than it sounds, but recognizing that His grace is sufficient is the first step of surrendering. Today I just ask you to recognize that with me. Ponder on the fact that His grace is sufficient.

Reflection:

Are you forfeiting grace, by putting your pride, your will, ahead of God in your life?

Application Step:

Memorize 2 Corinthians 12:9 ~ *But he said to me, "My grace is sufficient for you, for my power is made perfect in weakness." Therefore I will boast all the more gladly about my weaknesses, so that Christ's power may rest on me.*

Prayer:

Father God, help me surrender to you. Help me to stop trying to be all that I can be, and do all that I can do, and just be still and know that you are God. It's hard for me to let things go. I want to take control, to make things go my way. I want to earn the right to be called your child. But I know that's not how it works. Please forgive me for thinking that my way is better than your way. Help me to surrender all to you. Help me to remember that your grace is enough. Amen.

Enslaved

When the going gets tough...
Written by Heather Hart

Only be careful, and watch yourselves closely so that you do not forget the things your eyes have seen or let them slip from your heart as long as you live.
~Deuteronomy 4:9

I have been reading through Exodus this week, and I just can't get over how similar I am to the Israelites. No, I've never been a slave in Egypt, but I have been enslaved by sin, and I bet you have too. But you see, it's not just the part about being enslaved that reminds me of them. It's what comes after that. Just like the Israelites, when I realize that I'm trapped in sin, I cry out to God and ask Him to help me. But His answer, or the way He goes about things, isn't always what I expect. For the Israelites, God didn't just poof them to safety, He repeatedly sent plagues on Egypt, and it actually got worse for them before it got better. They didn't spend that time thanking God for hearing them. No, they spent it grumbling about how much worse it was. I do that too. When things happen that I don't understand, I don't always remember that God has a plan and is working things out for good. I get trapped in the here and now, just like the Israelites did.

Sadly, it doesn't end there. The Israelites didn't just eventually walk out of Egypt and never look back. They were fearful before crossing the sea, but God came through. They grumbled in the desert because they were without food and water, but God came through. They even spent time reminiscing about how much better their lives were when they were slaves, but God still came through for them.

Have you ever been there? When you're walking through your own desert of sin, do you ever look at God and grumble, or remember how some things were easier when you were enslaved to a sin. Maybe you're overcoming an eating disorder, or going through a breakup because you chose to stand up for your beliefs, or it could be something completely different. The bottom line is that I don't know what you're going through, but I do know that it's tempting to grumble against God, because I do it too. Being delivered from something we've been a slave to for a long time isn't easy. But if we learn anything from the Israelites, it should be that God comes through. We just have to trust that no matter what we are facing, He has a plan, and He will come through.

Reflection:

When the going gets tough, do you trust God to come through, or are you tempted to return to the slavery of sin?

Application Step:

Tell someone what you are going through. Whether it's a sin that you are still enslaved to, or something that you are in the process of being delivered through, God doesn't want you to be alone in the desert. Tell them about where you've been, and ask them to help you remember that God will be with you on this journey to freedom.

Prayer:

Father God, being enslaved to sin is no fun, but being delivered isn't always a walk in the park either. Help me to remember that no matter how tough the road to freedom may seem, you will come through. Help me to remember that you didn't abandon the Israelites in the desert, and you won't abandon me either. Help me to trust in you, Lord. Give me the strength I need to get through this. In the name of your Son and my Savior, I pray. Amen.

PMS

Mood swings 101
Written by Heather Hart

And God is able to make all grace abound to you, so that in all things at all times, having all that you need, you will abound in every good work.
~2 Corinthians 9:8

Every month around the same time, I get unbelievably cranky. I never remember why right away, but I have begun to see the pattern now. It's PMS. I don't know if those who surround you have to experience your wrath each month, but my family can tell you that it isn't a pleasant experience around here! I have been learning that even mood swings that are caused by my menstrual cycle can be controlled… it just takes a bit of work on my part, and <u>lot's</u> of grace from God. That's where today's verse comes in. Even when my body is suffering, God is able to make all grace abound to me. And if all grace can abound to me, it can abound through me - in all things and at all times… even during *that* time.

If you suffer from PMS like I do, I just want to encourage you today with God's grace. Because no matter what our physical body is going through, God loves us. He is more powerful than our hormones, our minstrel cycles, and any mood swing that comes our way. He can help us to overcome mood swings. He can help us display the fruit of His Spirit always, so that even when our hormones are raging, we can accomplish good works.

Reflection:

Do you let your hormones or the grace of God control your mood?

Application Step:

When you feel yourself starting to get worked up, ask God for His grace to abound to you and through you.

Prayer:

Father God, I admit that I don't always control my mood swings. I let my hormones run wild and play into the lie that they are stronger than your grace, but that isn't true. You are almighty, all powerful, and abounding in love for me. I know that with your help I can beat PMS, so today I ask you for that help. Help me to be kind and gentle, no matter what time of the month it is. Help me to bring honor to you, not let my hormones do damage to my witness for you. I ask this in the name of your Son, Jesus Christ. Amen.

Kindness

When being nice isn't easy...
Written by Heather Hart

I have set you an example that you should do as I have done for you.

~John 13:15

Being nice isn't always easy, that's all I could think about this morning when I was reading John 13. You see, this is the chapter where Jesus washed the disciple's feet, and it is very clear that Jesus knew at this point that Judas would betray Him...yet He washed his feet anyway. That couldn't have been an easy thing to do. After washing the feet of the man that would hand Him over to be killed, Jesus said the above words: *"I have set an example that you should do as I have done for you."* Does Jesus really want us to be nice to people that are mean to us? He surely didn't mean that if we knew someone started a rumor about us, stole our homework, or even threatened to beat us up, that we should still be nice to them! ...did He?

Well, to be honest, this wasn't the first time that Jesus had said something along those lines. It was recorded in Luke 6 that we are to love our enemies, do good to those who hate us, bless those who curse us, and pray for those who mistreat us (vs. 27-28). So yes, that's exactly what He meant. Surly if Jesus can wash the feet of the man who is going to hand Him over to be killed, He can help me muster up the humility to be kind to the girl who slept with my boyfriend last week.

Reflection:

Are you following Jesus' example of being nice, even when it isn't easy?

Application Step:

Think about a person that has done or said something mean to you or about you. Got it? Now think of a way that you can show them kindness today and go do so.

Prayer:

Heavenly Father, Jesus was an amazing human being. He still is amazing, but the example that He left for me to follow is unthinkable in today's standards. I need your help, God. If you really want me to follow the example that He left, I need your help. It is so hard to show kindness to those who trample on my feelings, to those who plot out ways to hurt me, God. But I want to be like Jesus, so I'm coming to you now. Help me to show kindness to everyone, even when it isn't easy.

Our Savior's Standing

Keeping up with the Jones'
Written by Heather Hart

...she gave birth to her firstborn, a son. She wrapped him in cloths and placed him in a manger, because there was no room for them in the inn.

~Luke 2:7

I was thumbing through my journal recently and found a note that I had jotted down last Christmas season. I was reading through the book of Luke and had come to rest on the above verse. It really struck me that Jesus didn't come to earth trying to 'keep up with the Jones'' so to speak. He came humbly. He was laid to rest in a manger. His first neighbors were literally animals. He didn't improve much from their either. He was raised by a poor family, and in His adult life he didn't even have a home of his own (Luke 9:58). Does that bother you? Our Savior didn't live in a 3 story home with a 2 car garage. He didn't wear designer clothes, or own a Ferrari. So why do we think we need to?

I don't know where you live, or what your standards are, but whether you live in a trailer or in a Beverly Hills mansion, I'm sure that you have either looked down on yourself, or someone else because of where they live or what they wear. Would you ever picture the girl wearing the ratty clothes eating lunch at a table with the girl who wears designer clothes? Probably not. But you know what? Christ would. He's the one that came humbly to save ALL of us. He doesn't care if your family has millions of dollars or if they are trying to scrape up enough change to buy dinner. He loves us where we are at. Why is it that we can't do the same?

Reflection:

Do you feel ashamed when your family doesn't have as much as the next, or do you look down on those who have less than you?

Application Step:

Whenever you get tempted to look at someone's material possessions, or financial standings, think of Christ. Picture that person (whether it's yourself or someone else) kneeling next to the crèche of Christ, and then ask yourself if it really matters what they are wearing, where they live, or what their family does for a living.

Prayer:

Father God, please forgive me for trying to keep up with the Jones'. It's so easy to look down on myself or others for not having as much as someone else, help me to remember that when I do that, that I'm looking down on you too, because you had even less than that. You didn't even have a home, Lord. You, the most amazing person ever born, were laid to rest in a barn. Help me to remember that when I get tempted to look at a material status. Help me to remember to look at the heart of a person, not what they wear, or what their parents do for a living. Help me to honor you, by not trying to keep up with the Jones'. Amen.

Sharing

What's mine is yours, and yours is mine
Written by Heather Hart

All the believers were one in heart and mind. No one claimed that any of his possessions was his own, but they shared everything they had.

~Acts 4:32

I just love to think about what it might have been like to be one of the first believers. Okay, well, once I get past the persecution part, the Bible says that they shared everything. None of the believers lacked anything, because they looked out for one another. Can you imagine what the world would be like if we still lived like that? Instead of having some families that lived paycheck to paycheck while others decided to buy a vacation house on the beach, having everyone have their basic needs met. Instead of trying to "keep up with the Jones'," we kept only what we needed and gave the rest to provide for the needs of others. Can you imagine that?

Would you be willing to trade your savings so that the girl from youth group could have a warm coat to get her through the winter? Would you give up your dream car so that the family down the street could pay for the insurance on their car? The people of the world would tell you how horrible of an idea that is, because we have to have savings and lookout for ourselves. We live in a world that has come down with a bad case of the "Mine-itis" as it's called on Sesame Street. But what would the world look like if we thought less about ourselves and protecting our possessions, and more about sharing and making sure that everyone had their needs met? I'd love to live in a world like that.

Reflection:

Do you have a case of "Mine-itis" where you lay claim to all of your possessions, protecting them at all costs? Or do you share everything that you have?

Application Step:

Whether you someone a gift, or just make a donation of one sort or another, find a way to share something today.

Prayer:

Father God, I admit that I don't share the way that your first followers did. It has been instilled in me that I have to lookout for myself, and that it's stupid to give things away without thought of where it will leave me. But that's not what your word says. It feels kind of childish to admit that I need to learn to share, but it's true. Please help me to get past the feeling of ownership, and remember that everything I have is yours. Help me to share what you have blessed me with with others, without thinking of myself. In the name of your Son, Jesus Christ, I pray this today. Amen.

Lonely

Created for Fellowship
Written by Heather Hart

"O Lord, you have seen this; be not silent. Do not be far from me, O Lord."

~Psalm 35:22

I find the above words so encouraging. Just to remember that the Lord sees us, He knows what we are going through, to remember that we are not alone – that's encouraging! However, I don't always remember those words. It seems that so often I feel alone. Like no one else understands what I'm going through. Do you ever feel that way? Like no one even cares? In today's world, I think it's easy to feel like that. And I bet a lot more people feel that way then are willing to admit it.

Things don't always go our way, things aren't always easy, and the people that surround us hurt us with their words and actions (intentionally or not). Life is rough. It's just that simple. When I feel all alone, I usually seclude myself even more. I couldn't explain why, but it seems like a natural response. It's like I want to be by myself, so that I can be lonely in peace. It sounds pretty silly to actually say that, but it's the truth. I can't help but wonder if that's exactly what Satan wants from us. If he plays on our emotions to seclude us from those who could encourage us, and help us to realize that we are not alone. Like Satan wants us to seclude ourselves to keep us protected from a world that cares – after all, if we seclude ourselves, it will be harder to see that we are wrong.

I don't know what trials you are going through, but I do know that life is rough. I also know that God sees us where we are. Satan may want us to stay secluded and lonely for as long as possible, but that's not what God wants. He built us for fellowship (Gen 2:18). When we seclude ourselves, we aren't pleasing God, but helping Satan to get a foothold on our minds. God wants us to encourage one another (1 Thessalonians 5:11), but when we hide away, we aren't letting others bring us that encouragement that God wants us to have – and we certainly aren't giving any encouragement to others.

Reflection:

When you feel alone, do you tend to seclude yourself, making it even worse in the long run?

Application Step:

Don't seclude yourself today. Whether that means not going straight to your room when you get home, or finding someone to eat lunch with, don't be alone. And while you're spending time with people, take the time to encourage someone else.

Prayer:

Father God, thank you for reminding me that you know where I am, and what I am going through. Thank you for always being near me, and for the reminder that you created me for fellowship. It's so easy to seclude myself when I'm feeling down, but that's not what you want for me. I know that now, Lord. I think I probably knew it all along, but it was just so easy. Please help me to find fellowship that is encouraging, God. Help me to encourage others, and to not put myself in a place where I will be tempted to shut others out. Amen.

Childlike Faith

Trusting the ultimate problem solver
Written by Heather Hart

Trust in the LORD with all your heart and lean not on your own understanding;
~Proverbs 3:5

Have you ever observed the way that babies interact with their parents? When they are hungry, they cry and they know that their mommies or daddies will feed them. As they grow older, and learn to talk, when they are hungry they go to their parents and simply tell them. Once again, they expect that their parents will see to it that their needs are met. But it's not just when they are hungry: anytime a small child has a problem, they turn to their parents. Whether their brother stole their toy or fell and scraped their knee, they know and trust, that their parents are capable to solve any problem that they come across. However, as we grow up, things change a bit. We start to lean on our own understanding. We start to trust ourselves, and eventually, we think we know more than mom and dad (wouldn't you agree?).

Today, while I was pondering on the above information, it really stuck with me that our spiritual growth sometimes resembles the latter instead of the former. Jesus said: *"I tell you the truth, anyone who will not receive the kingdom of God like a little child will never enter it."* (Luke 18:17). Yet we tend to spend our lives in the no-it-all phase when it comes to trusting Christ. Yes, we know He is there, we know that God is all-knowing, and we know that He is trustworthy, but we want to do it all on our own. Instead of trusting in the one we know is trustworthy, we lean on our own understanding... Sound familiar? We treat God the same way that we treat our parents, or at least I do. Instead of bringing my problems before God, and waiting for Him to tell me how to fix them, I simply keep trying on my own.

It's like trying to learn to swim without listening to your swimming instructor. The more I try to do it on my own, the more I sink. I sit their floundering, gasping for air, but I have too much pride to accept that I need help from my coach. Other times, it's like I already know how to swim, but I'm training for a race. Instead of listening to the one who can help me get better so that I can win, I trust that I am already good enough. When race day comes around, I end up in last place. Not because I wasn't capable of winning, but because instead of accepting the help I needed to get better, I trusted that I knew it all. Have you ever done that? Do you do that when your parents are trying to help you with your homework, or when you need help knowing how to handle any other problems? Whether we need help from our parents, our pastors, or our God, we have to learn not only to ask, but to accept help when it's offered... not just rely on our own knowledge and abilities. It's a hard lesson, but I think I'm learning. What about you?

Reflection:

Who is your trust in? Do you trust in yourself and lean on your own understanding, or do you put your trust and your faith in the one who made you?

Application Step:

Ask and accept help today. Whether that means praying to God for help, or just approaching your parents, stop leaning on your own understanding, and put your trust in Christ.

Prayer:

Father God, I owe you an apology. I have been trying to do things on my own; trusting in myself and my own abilities instead of in you. Please forgive me, Lord. Help me to have a childlike faith that trusts you to be my problem solver. Help me to stop being a little miss know-it-all, because that is the way that I have been acting. Lord, I need your help in this. I need your help to let go of my pride, and accept help from you, and from those that you have put in my life to help me…like my mom and dad. I ask these things in the name of your Son, Jesus Christ, today. Amen.

Filling the Void

Because even Jesus got hungry
Written by Kristie Evans

Early in the morning, as Jesus was on his way back to the city, he was hungry.

~ Matthew 21:18

Is it hard for you to think of our Savior as being hungry? For me, it is! I know He was human, but still, He really got hungry!? Well, yes, He did! And today, I want to say something about spiritual hunger: there really is a "void" in all of us - some say it's called a God shaped hole that only God Himself can fill. I just know that there is a place in us that does certainly feel empty, and we try to fill it with friends, family, sports, hobbies, shopping... just about anything and everything! But the thing is, we will continue to search until we find Jesus and ask Him in our hearts. When His spirit comes into our hearts, we are then saved.

What are we saved from? We are saved from death, hell, and the grave (eternal/spiritual death). We receive eternal life through the sacrifice of the life that Jesus gave on the cross. Way back, the people had to bring animal sacrifices to be forgiven of their sins. However, once Jesus made that one sacrifice of His own blood, He made atonement for you and for me. So, today we don't have to sacrifice animals. Thank you Jesus (I would be in serious trouble)!

Today, I want to ask you: Are you saved? Is Jesus your Lord? Are you ready for eternal life? All will stand before Him one day, and every knee will bow. The thing is, are you ready for that? Are you hungry for Jesus? Only He can fill that empty feeling/space that nothing else (and no one else) can. Seriously, are you hungry?

Reflection:

Have you accepted Christ as your Savior? Are you hungry for Him, or are you still trying to fill that hole inside of you with anything and everything else?

Application Step:

Spend some time reflecting on your life. What do you do when you feel empty? Do you turn to Christ, or to worldly passions? If it's the latter, pray for God to help you change that. If you have never invited Him into your life, now is the perfect time. If you do turn to Christ when you feel empty, spend time thanking Him for His goodness, and ask Him to continue to fill you to the brim with His spirit.

Also, consider memorizing Matthew 5:6 ~ *Blessed are those who hunger and thirst for righteousness, for they will be filled.*

Prayer:

Father God, thank you for this. It's something that I needed to hear. It doesn't matter if it's the first time, or the hundredth time, it's always good to be reminded and to think about the salvation that only comes from you. I ask you today, Lord, just to come into my heart and fill me full of your spirit. Nothing else will do, Lord. Nothing else can fill me the way that you do, because I was designed by you, and for you. I was created to be filled by you. Thank you for teaching me that. I pray that I always remember that it is you, and only you, that can fill me full of everlasting love. I pray today that you fill my cup, both now and forever. Help me to turn to you when I am empty; in the name of your Son, I pray. Amen.

A Fickle Follower

Are you a true friend?

Written by Heather Hart

Blessed are you when men hate you, when they exclude you and insult you and reject your name as evil, because of the Son of Man.

~Luke 6:22

Have you ever been left out of something just because you were a Christian or it violated your beliefs? Maybe your mom or dad told you that you couldn't go somewhere, or maybe you made the decision on your own. Either way, being left out is never fun. But you know what, while God doesn't rejoice in people hating us or leaving us out, but He does rejoice when we love Him enough to remain by His side no matter what. Think about it this way:

How would you feel if you had a friend that was only your friend when it was easy? Wouldn't you rather have a friend that stuck by you no matter what happened – through thick and thin? I sure would. But God is the same way. He doesn't want us to be fickle followers that are only Christians when it's easy. He says that we can either be true friends, or we're not really friends at all. Kind of like in real life huh?

So the next time that you are left out of something, or someone teases you about one of your beliefs, I encourage you to stand firm, and see God through.

Reflection:

Are you a fickle follower that is only a Christian when it's easy, or do you stand by God and His Word no matter what the cost?

Application Step:

The next time that you are asked to make a choice that you know goes against God's Word, chose to be a true friend, not a fickle follower. Then extend that to the rest of your relationships by choosing to stand by those in need, even when it's not easy or what you would really like to be doing (Do to others as you would have them do to you – Luke 6:31).

Prayer:

Father God, sometimes it's hard to make the decisions that I know are right. Taking the easy road is, well, easier. I don't want to be a fickle follower, Lord. I want to be true to you, no matter what the cost. Help me to do that in the future. Help me to remember that even if I get left out, or made fun of, that choosing to remain true to you is still the right decision. Thank you, Lord. In the name of your Son I pray, amen.

Promoting Love

Forgiveness vs. Gossip
Written by Heather Hart

He who covers over an offense promotes love, but whoever repeats the matter separates close friends.

~Proverbs 17:9

Have you ever had a friend hurt your feelings? I know I have. It's so tempting to run and tell everyone else what a horrible friend they are - to express our frustration. But that's not what God has called us to do. No, God has called us to love our friends enough to forgive them... and true forgiveness means not telling the world. It means covering the offence in love, and then letting it go.

Okay, I admit, I struggle with that - especially when it's not even a friend who hurts my feelings. What about when it's someone that we don't know or like? Are we still supposed to forgive them? According to God, yes. Proverbs 17:9 tells us that he who covers over an offense promotes love... God wants us to promote love. Not just to our friends, but to everyone. That was after all the lesson of the Good Samaritan wasn't it?

But forgiving isn't really the hard part. No, it's the next part of the verse that I struggle with: not repeating the matter... You know, when we get hurt, or someone offends us, it's almost natural to want to tell the world how we were wronged. We want to tell anyone who will listen that we have been offended! It doesn't matter who we want to tell, whether it's someone to get them into trouble (to separate close friends) or just someone to listen to us and feel sorry for us, God says that true forgiveness doesn't bring up the offense again.

Reflection:

When someone offends you, do you keep bringing it up, or do you cover over the matter with true forgiveness and love?

Application Step:

The next time you are tempted to tell someone about something bad that happened to you, ask yourself if you are promoting love, or trying to separate close friends with gossip.

Prayer:

Father God, controlling my tongue is hard work! When things go wrong, I just want to tell someone, but I know that I should be telling you, and you alone. Help me to learn to forgive and let live. Help me to remember that repeating the bad things doesn't make them better, but has the potential to cause more harm. Lord, I really need your help with this, so I ask in the name of your Son, Jesus Christ, amen.

The Sabbath

Real down time

Written by Heather Hart

And God blessed the seventh day and made it holy, because on it he rested from all the work of creating that he had done.

~Genesis 2:3

We are probably all familiar with the fact that God created the world in six days, and on the seventh day He rested. He blessed the seventh day, calling it the Sabbath and commanded it to be a day of rest. But I was wondering the other day, do we ever actually take real down time as He asked us to do? Do we ever go an entire day without turning on electronics, doing homework, housework, or any other kind of work? I'm not trying to get caught up in the logistics of it all; I just can't help but wonder if we ever REALLY take a day off. I have tried to, but it's so hard to unplug from life for an entire day. To make it possible, you really do have to FINISH your work in six days. That leaves the seventh day open for praising God. To be a day set apart for worshiping Him. Is it possible? Yes. But do we do it? – That is the real question.

Reflection:

Think for a minute: What would a true day of rest look like for you? What would it take to make it actually happen?

Application Step:

Make it happen! Even if it's just for one week, take an entire day off from doing work. Make sure that all of your homework and household chores are done the day before, and just spend an entire day resting and soaking in God's goodness.

Prayer:

Father God, you are amazingly smart. I need a day to just rest and recuperate from life, but in order to do that, I have to finish my work, just like you did. Help me to do that this week, Lord. Help me to get caught up on everything so that I can spend an entire day in your presence with nothing to distract me. In the name of your Son I pray, amen.

On Goals & Motivation

Where is your heart?
Written by Heather Hart

... Always give yourselves fully to the work of the Lord, because you know that your labor in the Lord is not in vain.
~1 Corinthians 15:58

During our lives, we set goals. That's just the way it is. We have dreams, desires, and destinations that we want to reach. Each one of those turns into a goal. We have a goal of reaching our dream job or desired pants size, but what is really the determining factor in whether or not we reach those goals, is our motivation. And motivation can come from two different places, selfish ambition or the desire to serve the Lord – and then there are days when it's just MIA. Today was one of those days for me, so I opened my Bible and started praying.

You see, God has a lot to say about motivation. He wants us to always give ourselves fully to His work as 1 Corinthians 15 says (vs. 58). He wants us to commit our ways to Him (Ps. 37:5), and seek first His kingdom and His righteousness (Matt. 6:33). God doesn't want us to grow weary of doing good (Gal. 6:9), but instead, seek to serve Him with all that we have (Luke 4:8). So on days like today when I feel unmotivated to get anything done, I bring myself back to this. To give myself fully to the work of the Lord, is to work even when I don't feel like it. When I start to grow weary of doing good, I have to trust in the Lord to renew my strength (Is. 40:31).

However, besides just being motivated to keep going when I feel weary, the list of Scriptures above also helps me check my motivation and goals. Is my dream job something that will honor God, or just a selfish ambition? God wants me to take care of my body and sometimes exercising and watching what I eat is part of that, but is starving myself to get to single digits really pleasing to God? You see, when my motivation doesn't come from the desire to do the work of the Lord, then my work is in vain. Sure, I might eventually reach my goal, but if it's not done for God, but done out of selfish ambition, then the Bible classifies my actions as evil (James 3:13-16).

Reflection:

Are you motivated by selfish ambition or by the thought of bringing glory to the Lord? Sit down and look at your goals, dreams or desires. Are they selfish, worldly goals?

Application Step:

Write down a few goals that aren't motivated by selfish ambition, and then look up the above Scriptures to help you stay motivated to reach those goals.

Prayer:

Father God, today I echo the words written in the Psalm 119 (vs. 28): "My soul is weary with sorrow; strengthen me according to your word." Lord, I don't feel very motivated, but I cling to the words of your prophet Isaiah: "those who hope in the LORD will renew their strength. They will soar on wings like eagles; they will run and not grow weary, they will walk and not be faint." Father God, even though I am weary and unmotivated, I know that you will renew my strength. I know that when I keep my focus on you, and serving you alone, that I can do anything. Help me to look to you for my motivation and my strength, and help me to be motivated to do things that bring glory to you. Align my goals with your will, O Lord. Amen.

Bad Hair Day

Refocusing on true beauty
Written by Heather Hart

Charm is deceptive, and beauty is fleeting; but a woman who fears the LORD is to be praised.
~Proverbs 31:30

I got my hair cut this week. I went in for a trim, and came out looking like Maria from the Sound of Music. I was not happy. I loved the hair cut that I had had prior to my "trim". But the lady just went too far, cut too much, and it didn't even look similar to what I had walked in with. I was devastated. The worst part was that it was so short, nothing short of shaving my head would get rid of the Sound of Music star that stared back at me when I looked into the mirror. While I hope that you never have to experience a bad haircut, we all have bad hair days at one time or another in our lives. I trust that you can understand the way I'm feeling to some degree. Think about it: when was the last time you had a bad hair day? Whether it was a hair cut gone bad, or a dye job that came out the wrong color, or even just a day when it wouldn't stay where you put it, or do what you wanted it to – I think we have all had bad hair experiences.

God has really been using this to teach me a little bit about true beauty. I guess you could say that prior to today, I have never really found much encouragement in today's verse. But it really does emphasize true beauty. You see, we can be nice to others, but still have a mean heart. We can be nice on the outside while critical on the inside. Being nice isn't being truly beautiful. Niceness comes and goes, but true beauty is eternal. Likewise, we can have the best haircut in the world, only to have someone ruin it in a matter of minutes. We can have the perfect complexion, just to wake up one morning with a zit. Why? Because true beauty isn't external. True beauty comes from fearing the Lord. Not being afraid of Him, but loving Him so much that you don't want to let Him down. So for the next few months, when I look in the mirror and see the happy nun looking back at me, I will remember that it isn't my haircut that makes me truly beautiful – it's the love that I have for God that really matters (and I really do love Him more than my hair... don't you?).

Reflection:

Are you more devastated when something happens to your external beauty, or when you do something that you know God doesn't like?

Application Step:

Spend some time today thanking God for your true beauty. Ask Him to help you focus more on the things that please Him (true beauty) then on your outer beauty that fades away (sometimes more quickly than others!).

Prayer:

Father God, I put more stock into my external beauty then I would care to admit. I don't want to keep living like this. I don't want my beauty to be only skin deep. Help me to grow in this, Lord. When something damages my external beauty, remind me to praise you for the fact that while external beauty is fleeting, true beauty lasts forever. Thank you for making me beautiful in you. Help me continue to grow more beautiful in Christ with each passing day, but keeping my focus on what really matters. I ask this in the name of Christ, amen.

The New Kid

Struggling to belong

Written by Heather Hart

By faith Abraham, when called to go to a place he would later receive as his inheritance, obeyed and went, even though he did not know where he was going.

~Hebrews 11:8

Have you ever read the story of Ruth? She moved to a new town where everybody hated her. They didn't like her simply because she came from somewhere else - She was different from them. Have you ever experienced that? Maybe your family moved and you have to go to a new school, maybe your just moving from middle school to high school, or maybe it's something else entirely, the point is that we all have to be the new kid at some point in our lives, and we won't always be accepted. Ruth is a perfect example of that. But she isn't the only example of that in the Bible. God called Abraham to be the new kid (Genesis 12:1). He actually spent most of his life roaming around in a place that didn't accept him. But you know what? God richly blessed both Ruth and Abraham. Abraham became the father of all believers, and Ruth was an ancestor of Jesus.

But, back to how that affects us... Life requires us to be the new kid from time to time. We move, or go to new schools, or join new teams – that's just life. Life is always changing, and sometimes it's easy to feel like an outcast. It's at times like that, when we have to remember that God can do mighty things with us in our new situations. Moreover, He doesn't want us to belong in this world (John 15:19). He wants us to be like Abraham, living our lives through faith, even if we end up feeling like an outcast. When we never have to experience becoming a new kid, we can get complacent, and start seeing life as all there is. We worry about what people think and say about us, but when we view life as something we are just passing through, when we acknowledge that we will be the new kid again before we know it (when we go to college, get a new job, or move again), when we focus on being who God wants us to be instead of who others expect us to be, that's when life is worth living.

Besides, who knows how God will use your new surrounding in your life. Maybe, like Ruth, you will meet your future husband. Or maybe, like Abraham, God will make your life better than you ever thought possible.

Reflection:

Do you live life like someone who belongs to the world, or someone who is following Christ, and waiting to settle down until you reach your eternal home?

Application Step:

Spend some time reflecting on whether you are struggling to belong to this world, or to Christ. Try memorizing John 15:19 this week to encourage you during the times when you feel like an outcast.

Prayer:

Father God, It's hard to feel like an outcast. I know that it wasn't easy for Abraham or Ruth, Lord, but you blessed them both so much! Help me to live by faith like Abraham. Help me to find encouragement in the story of Ruth. Lord, I want to live for you, not for the world. While it's tempting to want to go with the flow, and feel like I belong, I know that you want me to live my life as one set apart for your work. Help me to remember that I pray, amen.

Gentleness

Are you gentle?
Written by Heather Hart

Let your gentleness be evident to all. The Lord is near.
~Philippians 4:5

Gentleness is defined as being considerate, kind, and tender. Not harsh or severe, but mild and soft. Does that describe you? I have to admit, it doesn't always describe me very well. It's so easy to fall into sin - It's like our default setting. When I stop thinking about God, and concentrate only on myself, I get harsh... and quick. I really think it's because I stop focusing on what God wants, and only think about me, me, me. When I'm focused on myself it's easy to get upset when others do things that screw up my plans, but when I center my thoughts on Christ, when things go wrong it's much easier to respond in kindness, remembering that Christ came to save an imperfect world, not a perfect one.

That brings me to today's verse, I absolutely love the way it's written. Paul starts out by encouraging us to be gentle, and ends by redirecting our thoughts to remind us that God is near. That really just helps to remind me that I can't be gentle when I'm focused on myself. Gentleness is a fruit of the spirit (Gal. 5:22-23), not a fruit of selfishness... Thus, I can't be gentle if I'm not focused on Christ.

Reflection:

Do you ever tend to get harsh because you are focusing on yourself and your plans instead of on God and what He has done?

Application Step:

The next time you realize that you are lacking in the gentleness department, stop and ask yourself where your focus is. Then, if necessary, redirect your focus onto the fact that God is near, and make sure that your attitude is pleasing to Him.

Prayer:

Father God, I tend to be a very selfish person at times, and that makes me lash out at others instead of letting the fruit of gentleness be evident... can you help me to work on that? I want to focus more on you, and less on me, but I need your help. So, I ask this in the name of your Son, Jesus Christ, amen.

Praying Together

When we pray for you...
Written by Heather Hart

We always thank God, the Father of our Lord Jesus Christ, when we pray for you,
> ~Colossians 1:3

When I picked up my Bible this morning to start reading, I didn't get very far before I had to stop and think about the above verse. Paul was writing to the church in Colossae from prison, he was there with a few other people and they had been praying... *together*. It just made me stop and wonder when the last time that I actually prayed *with* someone was. Not for them, or sat there while one person prayed for a group of us, but actually prayed together? Could you answer that question? To be quite honest, it's been a while for me. I pray by myself all the time, but community prayer... not so much. We take the time to let one person pray for our food before meals, but that's not really praying together... it's having one person thank God while the rest listen. Don't get me wrong, there are lots of opportunities to pray with my friends and family – we could pray together before bed, in the car, on the phone, before school or work... the list is endless – so why don't we?

I have to admit, the Bible has a ton to say about praying together: Acts 1:14 and 4:24, 2 Corinthians 13:7, Colossians 1:9, 1 Thessalonians 1:2, and 2 Thessalonians 1:11 just to name a few, but the list just keeps going. So I have to think that praying together is pretty important, after all Paul surely thought it was and he wrote a good portion of the New Testament! Now, to go and do likewise...

Reflection:

When was the last time that you prayed *with* someone?

Application Step:

Pray *with* someone today. Whether it's with your mom or dad, a friend at school, or even over the phone with someone you talk to today, make sure that you take the time to join together in prayer *with* someone.

Prayer:

Father God, I like talking to you. Prayer is one of my favorite things, but I don't often do it with anyone. It's more of a private thing for me. I realized today that you really want me to pray with other people, not just for them. That's going to be hard for me, Lord, so I'm asking you for help. Give me the strength to open up my faith in you, and share it with those around me through prayer. In the name of your Son I pray this today, amen.

Be Yourself

"The Comparison Trap"
Written by Shelley Hitz

Lift up your eyes and look to the heavens: Who created all these? He who brings out the starry host one by one and calls forth each of them by name. Because of his great power and mighty strength, not one of them is missing.
~Isaiah 40:26

You know, often many of us get caught up in what we sometimes call the comparison trap. We could be comparing our appearance or our abilities to others – you know how it goes. It's easy to compare ourselves with others, and this week I found myself getting caught up in that comparison trap. For instance, this last week, my husband and I went jogging with a group of runners. It was the type of thing that wasn't a race, but we were just getting together to jog and then you got a free gift if you showed up. So, I'm not a big runner like my husband is, but I thought, *"Oh hey, a free gift, I'll go too."*

When we got there, I was one of the last ones. I'm so slow, and I was feeling not as good as the other people. And I just felt like God began to tell me, *"You know Shelly, you should be thankful that you're even out here running. You know, be grateful that you have the ability to do that, and that you even got up out of your couch to come."* And you know, I was able to spend that time with Jesus, He was my running partner. And my attitude began to change. But, you know, when I get focused on myself it's so easy to feel inferior - or to feel less than - when I start comparing myself with others. It seems like we often compare our weaknesses to other peoples' strengths, so it makes us feel so inferior.

Another example was this week when I was comparing myself to another speaker. This speaker gets a lot more bookings then I do and is a lot more popular, and it's so easy to feel inferior that I'm not as good as that person. And I feel like God was just reminding me, _be yourself,_ _because everyone else is already taken._ I loved that! I need to be me - I need to be Shelley Hitz. I need to be who God has created _me_ to be. Because you know what, everyone else is already taken anyways, and God has gifted me just like He's gifted you; with gifts and abilities that are individual to us - that are unique to us. We're all part of the body of Jesus Christ, as Christians - Christ followers. We all have a unique roll and God wants each one of us to embrace that.

Reflection:

Are you stuck in the comparison trap, or are you free to be you?

Application Step:

Spend some time writing down a list of your strengths. Then whenever you start to compare yourself to someone else, remind yourself that God created each of us uniquely and focus on your strengths instead of your weaknesses.

Prayer:

Father God, it seems so easy to look at other people and see all of the things that they can do better than I can – all of the things that they are excelling at while I stumble. Please help me to remember that you created me to be me. Lord, you created each star to shine differently. Help me to remember that you created each person the same way, and have gifted me with my own strengths. Remind me that if I try to be like someone else, that I will end up being the one that is missing. In the name of your son, I pray; amen.

Leftovers

When the best is gone, but there's still something left

Written by Heather Hart

In the course of time Cain brought some of the fruits of the soil as an offering to the LORD.

~Genesis 4:3

You know the story of Cain and Able, right? They were Adam and Eve's first children and one ended up murdering the other? Yeah, that one. Well, I think that there are times when I am more like Cain then Able Now don't get me wrong, I've never killed anyone! I don't relate to Cain in that way, but with the offering part of it: Able brought God an offering from his best; the first of his flock. Cain... yeah he brought some. He didn't forget about God, but he didn't make Him a first priority either. Can you relate to that? I sure can. There are lots of times when I bring God some. I don't forget, but I don't give Him my all either. I certainly don't give Him the best that I have to give... He tends to get stuck with the leftovers. He gets what's leftover on Sunday morning I after I have exhausted myself by getting ready for church and bickering with my family. He gets what's leftover from the day each night before I go to bed. He gets the leftover money that I have in my purse when the offering plate passes by... Well, you get the picture.

Reflection:

What about you? Do you give God your best (like Able) or your leftovers (or just some like Cain)?

Application Step:

Make the decision to give God your best this week. Whether that means skipping a T.V. show to spend time with God when you are more awake, intentionally saving money to put in the offering, or something else entirely - just do it.

Prayer:

Father God, I need to ask you to forgive me. It's kind of scary to think of myself like Cain, but it's true. I'm selfish. I have been putting myself before you, and I am so sorry. You have been getting the leftovers from my life, and you deserve so much more than that. Help me to do better at putting you first. Help me to give you my best, not what's left. In Jesus name I pray; amen.

Thrive

Are you merely surviving or are you thriving?

Written by Shelley Hitz

The thief comes only to steal and kill and destroy; I have come that they may have life, and have it to the full.
~John 10:10

This morning when I went to get into the shower we had a little water pressure issue. If we flush the toilet right before we take a shower, it really dramatically decreases the water pressure in the shower. So, you have to wait a few minutes and eventually it comes back. Well, today I was kind of in a rush so I just jumped into the shower, waiting for the water pressure to come back on. Well, I was able to survive in the shower: I washed my face, I was finally able to wet my hair, but it just wasn't the same because it was just kind of a trickle of water. I just kept thinking when is it going to come back full blast? You know, it just seemed to take longer today. Finally, just as I was thinking that, boom, the water came back on and it was just like oh, this is amazing! I was just barely surviving, but now I was thriving. I just stood there and enjoyed the warm shower for a while - Before, I was just trying to get it done as quickly as possible.

That image brought back to me the idea of our spiritual lives and how sometimes we just get by -we just survive. Maybe there is stuff in your life that is sucking away your water pressure, so to speak, and your spiritual life. Like that toilet was sucking away the water pressure of my shower. Maybe it is a boyfriend who is kind of pulling you away from Christ. Maybe it is some friends or maybe it is stuff on the internet or some music you are listening to. Maybe it is some girls you have gotten caught up in some sexting stuff or maybe it is some webcam things you have been doing. Maybe it is just your thoughts. Maybe it is some depression or some low self-esteem, but it is just sucking some of the life out of you. You just feel life is just like a little trickle and you can survive on that. You can get by, but it just feels like there is meant to be more. You just keep wondering when are things going to change in my life. When I am going to have that full life that Christ intended for me? If you are follower of Jesus Christ, He promised in the Bible in John 10:10 saying, "I have come to give life and life abundantly." Life to the full. He didn't mean for us just to barely get by. He meant for us to thrive.

I was also thinking of the verse in Revelation in Chapter 3, verse 15, "I know your deeds that you are neither cold nor hot. I wish you were either one or the other so because you are lukewarm, neither hot nor cold, I am about to spit you out of my mouth." It is just that image of being lukewarm, of just surviving, of getting by in life but not really having that full life that God has intended for us to be hot spiritually, so to speak. Then, also, in Revelation in Chapter 2, verse 4, it says,

"Yet I hold this against you. You have forsaken your first love." So many times we allow other things to come in first place in our lives. For those of us who are followers of Jesus, we forsake our first love of Jesus. It is so easy to do.

Reflection:

I just want to ask you today if there is something that is dragging you down. Are you merely surviving or are you thriving?

Application Step:

I encourage you today. If there is something in your life, bring it to God. Ask him for forgiveness and He will bring that in your life. Jesus has so much more for us. He has life and life abundantly.

Prayer:

Father God, please forgive me. I have been bogged down by the things of this world. I don't want to keep merely surviving, I want to thrive! I come to you now and ask that you help me change. Help me to be different, God. Help me to turn from the burdens of this world, to stop letting the things of this life zap my energy and ability to thrive, Lord, and help me turn to you. Empower me to change, God, and show me what to do.

Lighting the Way

Hey, who turned out the lights?

Written by Heather Hart

When Jesus spoke again to the people, he said, "I am the light of the world. Whoever follows me will never walk in darkness, but will have the light of life."

~John 8:12

Have you ever gotten up in the middle of the night and tried to walk through your pitch black bedroom, only to step on or trip over something that you forgot was on the floor? Okay, so even if your cleaning skills are better than mine, I'm sure you can imagine having something like that happen. I mean, we all know that it's hard to walk in the dark because we simply can't see where we are going, and that makes it hard to know when to step over or around an obstacle in our path. Life is so much easier when we turn on the lights!

That's what I think Jesus meant when He said that He was the light of the world. Trying to go through life on our own, is like fumbling around in the dark; we have to try to figure out what's best for us and know when to say yes or no, or when to act, and when to wait. Trying to figure life out by ourselves is a pretty daunting task! But God already knows what's best for us, and He sent Jesus to light the way. Sure, we can choose to try a different way, but without the light of Christ, we will continue stumbling in the dark. I don't know about you, but whenever I try to do things on my own and set off into the darkness, I almost always wind up flat on my face. I need the light of Christ to see life clearly. We all do. When we have Christ lighting our way, and take Him at His word, we have that lighted path. We can walk through anything, because we can see where we are going. Even if we can't see around a corner, at least we won't walk into the wall.

Reflection:

Are you following Jesus everyday/all the time, or are you walking around without the lights on?

Application Step:

Spend some time today studying your road map (God's Word) and remember to acknowledge Christ as you go about your day – Be sure to keep the light on.

Prayer:

Father God, thank you for sending Jesus to light up my life. Life is so hard, I don't know what I would do if I had to go through it in the dark. Help me to remember to look to you when things get tough. When the darkness of the world starts to crowd in Lord, help me to remember that you are with me and are lighting the way, I just need to go towards the light. Continue to guide me, I pray. Amen.

Witnessing

Because we would want to know...
Written by Shelley Hitz

Very truly I tell you, whoever hears my word and believes him who sent me has eternal life and will not be judged but has crossed over from death to life.

~John 5:24

Do you like to go shopping? I know I do. Now imagine that your favorite store is having a 99% off sale. Not only that, but that it's at 2:30 in the morning. Would you set your alarm to go? I know I would. Now what if all of your friends knew about the sale - all of them went, they set their alarms - and they got a ton of stuff. But what if they never told you? You were in bed sleeping while this sale was going on! How would you feel? Would you feel a little bit disappointed? Maybe a little bit upset, maybe even a little bit angry? 'Why didn't they tell me?!' 'Why did they keep this to themselves?!'

Well, I want to tell you that I feel like I have found a 99% off sale. The things that God has done in my heart and in my life in these past few years have been literally amazing: The brokenness that I was in - the despair - just the emotions and the place that I was at. God has brought so much healing and hope, and He has brought restoration to my life. I feel like at this point I can't not tell you about it. Because it's just like that 99% off sale, someday you may think, 'Shelley, why didn't you tell me?!'

Have you ever thought about it that way before? We wouldn't keep a 99% off sale at our favorite store from our friends, so why do we keep God's 100% off sale from them? How can we not tell them that our sins are so expensive that we have to pay for them with eternity in hell, but God is having a sale – a 100% off sale? That He sent His Son to pay for our sins, so we can live eternally with Him for FREE? That's a pretty awesome sale. Probably the best sale in all of history wouldn't you say? So why don't we let others in on it?

Reflection:

Do you tend to hold back from telling your friends about what God has done for us – for them? One day will both you and they look back wishing that you would have told them?

Application Step:

Find a way to tell one of your non-Christian friends or family members about Christ our Savior this week. It doesn't matter if you sit down and have a heart to heart, post a Facebook update, or even give them a Bible, just take the time to let them know what God has done.

Prayer:

Father God, once again I come to you to ask for your forgiveness. I've been selfish by keeping what you have done to myself. I don't know why it's so hard to let my friends know about the amazing things that you have done, but it is. Help me to get past that, Lord. Help me to share your good news with them. Don't let me keep something this important from them any longer. I pray that you give me strength to move forward. Amen.

Not Shaken

When things start to crumble...
Written by Shelley Hitz

"'Though the mountains be shaken and the hills be removed, yet my unfailing love for you will not be shaken nor my covenant of peace removed,' says the LORD, who has compassion on you."

~Isaiah 54:10

Today, I want to talk to you about being shaken. What does that exactly mean? I'm not talking about someone coming over and physically shaking you, but I'm talking about being emotionally shaken, spiritually shaken, or shaken up by peer pressure. Yesterday I was feeling kind of shaken - I was just feeling sick, I had a lot of things that I wanted to do, and I just didn't feel like doing anything. And as I was doing my time with the LORD in the morning, I came across Today's verse. Isaiah 54:10 says, *"'Though the mountains be shaken and the hills be removed, yet my unfailing love for you will not be shaken nor my covenant of peace removed,' says the LORD, who has compassion on you."*

Several years ago I was reading that verse and I was just praying over it and just visualizing what that might mean for me at that time. And I remember that at that time that verse just came alive to me, and that came back to me yesterday. The picture that I got was of an earthquake happening and everything all around me being shaken and destroyed, and just taken down to rubble. Yet, this verse specifically says, *"Though the mountains be shaken and the hills be removed... my unfailing love for you will not be shaken."* I just got this picture that all around everything else is in destruction, and yet there was one building standing strong - one building that was not impacted, that was not shaken by that earthquake. It was the building of God's love for me, and that it would always stand, no matter what would happen, what would come of my life. I've had a lot of things happen in my life, but God has been that stable force for me and yesterday I needed that reminder.

I want to close with Psalm 62:1-5, these are some of my favorite verses. It says, *"My soul finds rest in God alone; my salvation comes from him. He alone is my rock and my salvation; he is my fortress. I will never be shaken. How long will you assault a man? Would all of you throw him down- this leaning wall, this tottering fence? They fully intend to topple him from his lofty place; they take delight in lies. With their mouths they bless, but in their hearts they curse."* And then again, *"Find rest, O my soul, in God alone; my hope comes from him."*

Reflection:

So I want to ask you today, are you feeling shaken? Or are you feeling secure in God?

Application Step:

Memorize Psalm 16:8 ~ *"I have set the LORD always before me. Because he is at my right hand, I will not be shaken."*

I encourage you to find that security in God, to repeat to yourself, and to remind yourself, "I will not be shaken." - When you feel like kids are making fun of you, or you feel like you're having a bad day, or your getting peer pressured to give in and compromise what you believe, when you're getting pressured to have sex with your boyfriend, and your wanting to fight with your brothers and sisters, your parents or just those things that tend to shake us, or whether you're just going through a really dark time, I just encourage you, to just repeat to yourself, "I will not be shaken." And it's because the LORD is always before you. It's because He is with you. And He will never leave you.

Prayer:

Father God, thank you for being there for me as my strong tower. Thank you that no matter what is going on around me, I can know that you and your love for me stand firm. Help me to remember that when I start to feel shaken. Amen.

When I Fail...

He brings me back
Written by Heather Hart

"I'm going out to fish," Simon Peter told them, and they said, "We'll go with you." So they went out and got into the boat, but that night they caught nothing.

~John 15:3

The pastor at my church preached a very powerful message last week at church. He was preaching on John 15 when Jesus came to meet the disciples when they were fishing after His resurrection, and he gave me an entirely new way to think about it. You see, the disciples were supposed to be in Galilee waiting for Jesus, but instead, they were fishing. Why? They felt like failures as disciples. They had turned away from Christ when He needed them the most, and they thought He was dead anyway, so they were throwing in the towel so to speak. Instead of pressing forward, they looked back and remembered that they use to be fishermen, so they went back to that - But they didn't catch any fish because that wasn't what God wanted them to do. In fact, Jesus didn't get mad that they didn't do what they were told, instead He came and met them where they were – and He does that for us too.

There are so many times in life that I have tried to choose my own path. Maybe I didn't feel qualified for what God wanted me to do, or maybe I just thought my own way was better, either way, instead of doing what God wanted, I did something else entirely. And you know what? Each and every time when my plan is failing and nothing is going the way that I want it to, God comes and brings me back to Him. He meets me where I am, someplace that He told me not to go, and He loves me anyway – just like He did for the original disciples. He's a pretty awesome God like that.

Reflection:

Do you tend to do the things that you feel comfortable and qualified to do, or do you drop everything to follow Christ?

Application Step:

If things aren't going your way today, remember that no matter where you are, God's not far away and He's willing to meet you where you are. But also, when you have to make decisions, remember that God has already told us where to go and how to live, and if we choose our own way, there's a good possibility that things won't go the way we want them to...

Prayer:

Father God, sometimes I feel like a failure when it comes to serving you. I look at my life, and what you have called me to do, and I see all of the ways that I've messed up. Sometimes it looks like it would be easier just to throw in the towel. Satan is right there taunting me that I will never be good enough, so why keep going. That's why I found so much encouragement in Jesus meeting the disciples by the sea shore. So often I am just like them. Failing you and life all at the same time, and it's just amazing to remember that even when I'm a failure, you love me anyway. Even when I go the wrong way and screw everything up, you will meet me where I am. Thank you for that.

Life's Lemonade

When Life Gives You Lemons...
Written by Heather Hart

And we know that in all things God works for the good of those who love him, who have been called according to his purpose.

~Romans 8:28

Earlier this week, a friend of mine posted a status update that I just loved. She said that several not so good things had happened to her during the week, and she didn't always have the best attitude about them. However, she felt like God was just saying to her, "When given lemons, make lemonade."

Have you ever wondered where that saying came from, or if it was biblical? Well, that's what my friend was wondering on that particular day and I have been wondering about it too. It seems like the Bible is just full of stories where the lemons of life are turned into lemonade! Think about it. Joseph's brothers sold him into slavery and he was unjustly thrown into jail (lemons!), but God used it for good and he ended up being a hero (lemonade). Balak hired Balaam to curse the Israelites (lemons), but God turned it into a blessing instead (lemonade). Even our Savior was beaten and put to death on the cross (lemons!) but through that came our sweet salvation (lemonade).

But God didn't just turn life's lemons into lemonade in the Bible; no, He does it in our lives too. For instance, my mom is a teacher and the school that she taught at got closed down last year (lemon) but they offered her a teaching job at a different school that paid their teachers more so she ended up getting a raise (lemonade!). My dad is an over-the-road truck driver which means he is hardly ever home (lemon!), but all of the kids that still live at home get to go on the truck with him each summer, just them and dad traveling across the US (lemonade!). I had cancer when I was a little girl (lemon!), but God has used the impact that that left on my life to make me into who I am today, and when my own little baby boy was born with cancer God used the wisdom from my own experience to get me through that time (lemonade).

Reflection:

When life gives you lemons, do you suck up the lemon juice and make a sour face, or do you let God use those lemons to make sweet lemonade out of your life?

Application Step:

Make a list of some of the lemons in your life that have been turned to lemonade, or could be if you let them.

Prayer:

Father God, I'm so grateful that you know how to make lemonade out of lemons. Please help me not to suck up the sour juices of life's lemons before you have a chance to turn them into a sweet, refreshing drink. Help me to look to you when lemons are thrown my way, so that I can taste and see your lemonade of life. Amen.

Ageism

Don't let anyone look down on you for being young
Written by Shelley Hitz

"Don't let anyone look down on you because you are young, but set an example for the believers in speech, in life, in love in faith, and in purity."

~ 1 Timothy 4:12

As a teenage girl, have you ever felt like someone looks down on you because you are young? Well I'm no longer a teenager, I am 35 years old, and yet I have that desire to be respected as an adult who has been through a lot and who God is pouring into and sharing with others. Yet, sometimes when I go to speak somewhere because I look so young it bothers me and I feel rejected. I feel like people look at me and think oh, what does she have to say or what could she tell us because she's so young. I can't even explain it – my husband just thinks it's crazy - but I don't like it.

As a teenager, have you ever felt that way? That somebody looks down on you? Oh, what does she have to tell us or how could she have anything to offer. She is only a teenager. And, yet God thinks differently. He sees things differently. You know, God was reminding me of this the other day. There is a verse in 1 Timothy 4:12. You may be familiar with it. It says, *"Don't let anyone look down on you because you are young, but set an example for the believers in speech, in life, in love in faith, and in purity."*

Recently, I went to go speak at women's brunch. It was a great event with beautiful women. There was a woman who came up to me ahead of time and she was like, "Oh, are you Shelley?" I said yes, and she said, "Oh, I just thought you would be so much older, you know, I didn't think you would be so young." And, then there it is again. The enemy, who is Satan or the devil, likes to plant lies in our minds and likes to get us to feel inferior, or less than, or think people are judging us. So, it went right into that thought in my mind. It was like 'oh, she is judging me, looking down upon me. She thinks I have nothing to offer and maybe I don't, what am I doing here, why am I speaking here?' A torrent of thoughts came into my mind and that the enemy was placing them in my mind. So, I went on to say, "Well, how old do you think I look?" She said, "Oh, maybe 20." I said, "Well, actually, I'm 35." She responded, "Oh really, oh my goodness, duh, duh..."

Well, I was getting ready to speak. I'm sitting there thinking okay, Lord, I'm really feeling like these women are judging me, looking at me and don't want to hear from me because I look young. I know that was a lie. I mean it sounds absurd to even say it now, but I was feeling those things. I was feeling insecure. I was feeling the insecurity. Sometimes you may feel that way, too.

I was feeling that way and all of a sudden God brought this verse to my mind. That's the power of memorizing scripture. I don't know when I memorized this scripture. It was probably a long time ago when I first memorized it, but it came right back to my mind. "Don't let anyone look down on you because you are young, but set an example for the believers in speech, in life, in love, in faith and in purity." I don't even know if I recited it word for word exactly, but it came back to me and I kept repeating that in my mind. Don't let anyone look down on you because you are young. I was thinking Lord, it's not about me. It is not about me at all. It is about you and your Holy Spirit working through me, speaking through me. God worked a miracle in my life. He took that insecurity away. He took those lies away in His power and through His word, His truth, He broke the power of those lies.

So, I got to speak and God was there. His Holy Spirit spoke powerfully. And do you know what? Afterward so many people came up to say things to me, but you know who gave me the biggest encouragement afterward? It was the same lady who I felt discouraged by ahead of time. I thought the enemy was trying to use her words to discourage me and yet afterward, God was using her to encourage me. She said, "You are doing exactly what you are supposed to do. It was so powerful and just amazing." The irony of it. Yet, that's what can happen sometimes when we believe the lies of the enemy and we get trapped in that. It can steal, kill and destroy from us.

Reflection:

Do you ever let other people discourage you because of your age (or how old you look)?

Application Step:

Don't let anyone look down on you because you are young, but set an example for the believers in speech, in life, in love, in faith, and in purity. That's 1 Timothy 4:12, and I encourage you to repeat it to yourself whenever you start to feel discouraged because of your age.

Prayer:

Father God, thank you for today's verse. For reminding me that age isn't really as important as following our calling to obey you. Please remind me of this verse when people start to look down on me because of my age. Help me to remember that to you age doesn't matter, but how I live my life, and the example that I provide to others. In the name of your Son, Jesus Christ, I pray today. Amen.

Purity

Keeping your fire in the fireplace
From the book *Mirror Mirror* by Shelley Hitz

"Marriage should be honored by all, and the marriage bed kept pure, for God will judge the adulterer and all the sexually immoral."

~ Hebrews 13:4

Imagine your house has a fireplace to provide heat in the cold winter months. Well, let's say that your parents asked you to start a fire when you got home from school. What if you decided to start the fire in the middle of your bedroom instead of in the fireplace? Would your parents come home and think everything was normal? Of course not. And what would be the consequences? You could literally burn your entire house down and be homeless within hours! Talk about being left out in the cold!

Well, our fire of sexual passion is also designed for the fireplace, the fireplace of marriage. If our sexual passion is let loose outside the boundaries of a committed marriage, it will leave damage (broken hearts, depression, STD's, pregnancy, etc.)....just like the damage that would occur if you started a fire in the middle of your bedroom instead of in your fireplace at home. What is the moral of this story? **Keep your fire in the fireplace!**

Most of us know that God forbids sexual intercourse outside of marriage. I Corinthians 6:18-20 says, *"Flee sexual immorality. All other sins a man commits are outside his body, but he who sins sexually sins against his own body. Do you not know that your body is a temple of the Holy Spirit, who is in you, whom you have received from God? You are not your own; you were bought at a price. Therefore honor God with your body."*

But knowing where everything else fits into God's standards is where the lines become gray.

*"Be imitators of God, therefore, as dearly loved children and live a life of love, just as Christ loved us and gave himself up for us as a fragrant offering and sacrifice to God. But among you **there must not be even a hint of sexual immorality**, or of any kind of impurity, or of greed, because these are improper for God's holy people...For this you can be sure: **No immoral, impure or greedy person - such a man is an idolater - has any inheritance in the kingdom of Christ and of God.**"* Ephesians 5:2-3,5

This is serious stuff - nothing to play around with. If you misunderstand what it means to be sexually immoral, you may risk missing out on the inheritance of the kingdom of God. *Not even a hint.* I know I have not always lived my life according to this standard. How about you?

Reflection:

Are you committed to saving your sexual passion for the right place at the right time (the fireplace of marriage), or are you playing with a fire and risking the chance of being burnt (both now and in eternity)?

Application Step:

If you haven't already, make the commitment today to save the fire of your sexual passion for marriage. It doesn't matter how far you've gone already, you can still choose to make the right decisions from here on out. Consider getting yourself a purity ring as a reminder (you can get a cheap ring at Walmart for under $10).

Prayer:

Father God, in today's world, it's easy to forget how dangerous it is to play with sexual fire. Thank you for the reminder of how important it is to you. From this day forward, I want to save my fire for the fireplace. Help me to do that, Lord. Help me to stay pure for you, for me, and for my future husband. In the name of your Son I pray; amen.

Jesus-chute

The Eternal Life Saver
Written by Shelley Hitz

For we must all appear before the judgment seat of Christ, so that each of us may receive what is due us for the things done while in the body, whether good or bad.
~2 Corinthians 5:10

Let's imagine you are getting on a plane. Some of you may have flown on a plane recently, but let's say you are getting on an airplane to get from point A to point B. The flight attendant hands you this backpack and says, "This is a parachute. It is going to make your flight more comfortable." You are like, "Cool. Thank you so much!" You put the backpack on and you go to your seat. Pretty soon, this lump in your back starts feeling uncomfortable and it starts getting hot. People start looking at you and laughing and making jokes like, "Oh my goodness, can you believe she is wearing that backpack?!" Then the flight attendant walks by, trips and spills coffee on you. You think 'this is not making my flight more comfortable at all!' So, what do you do? You take it off and put it under the seat thinking that the attendant lied - It didn't make your flight more comfortable.

Now, let's consider a second scenario. Let's say you get on the plane and the flight attendant gives you that backpack with the parachute and says, "Here, this has a parachute in it. You will need it. At some point during this flight, we are going to have to make a 25,000-foot jump. If you don't have this backpack, you won't make it. You will die." So, you put that backpack on thinking 'oh, my goodness, I need to be ready. I have a 25,000-foot jump ahead.' You go to your seat and that lump is in your back and you are feeling kind of uncomfortable, but you don't care. You're not taking off that backpack because you know you need it. It starts getting hot, people start making fun of you – ha, she is still wearing the backpack. Why does she wear it now? That is so dumb. They are just making fun of you, but you still will not budge. You are keeping that backpack on no matter what happens.

So, what was the difference between scenario one and scenario two? Well, scenario one is where the flight attendant told you it was going to make your flight more comfortable whereas scenario two you were told the purpose of why you need to keep it on. It is for the jump ahead.

Some people might tell you to put Jesus Christ on – to try out a relationship with Jesus because He will make your life better, and so you may for a season try out Jesus. Thinking "Let's see if He truly does make my life better." Now, Jesus does give us his Holy Spirit and His Holy Spirit is love, joy, peace, patience, kindness, goodness. All kinds of great gifts God gives us. He does fill us to the full and He does give us satisfaction, but it doesn't necessarily mean that life is going to get better or that it is going to be easy or more comfortable, so to speak. So, someone tells you to try Jesus because He will make your life (or your "flight" more comfortable). You may have a tendency to want to put Him off when you feel that lump in your back or people start making fun of you or hard times come. But there is a reason that we should put Jesus on: it's because there is a jump ahead, a 25,000-foot jump and it is called "Judgment Day". Today's verse says, "For we must all appear before the judgment seat of Christ that each one may receive what is due him for the things done while in the body, whether good or bad." You see, we are all going to have to stand before Jesus one day when we die or if we are still alive when Jesus comes back when He returns to this earth for His people. We are going to have to stand before Him and give an account for the things we have done during this life whether good or bad. If we don't come to Christ, if we don't ask for forgiveness and have true repentance in our lives, then we won't be ready and we may end up in eternity in hell. Hebrews 9:27 to 28 says, "Just as a man is destined to die once and after that to face judgment so Christ was sacrificed once to take away the sins of many people. He will appear a second time not to bear sin but to bring salvation to those who are waiting for Him."

The Bible says in John 16:33, "In this world you will have trouble." It doesn't say might or maybe – it says you will have trouble but take heart I, Jesus, have overcome the world. So, are you ready for that jump ahead? I hope so.

Reflection:

Are you waiting for Him? Have you put on that parachute of Jesus Christ, the blood of Jesus that was shed for you?

Application Step:

I encourage you to take what I call the "good test" on my website. It is on the left-hand side and there is a link to it. Take that test and read the entire next page. See if you are ready. See if you have that parachute on. If you have truly repented and truly changed, your life will change because it is just not to make your life better.

Prayer:

Father God, thank you for reminding me that Jesus isn't just some cool trend that's there to make life grand. He came and died so that I could live. Thank you for that. Thank you for sending Him to die for my sins. Thank you for giving me an eternal life saver that will be the only thing that makes a difference on Judgment day. Having Jesus as a life saver is the only thing that has the power to keep me safe; I know that, and I am ever so grateful. Thank you, Lord. Amen.

Conclusion

We hope that you have enjoyed this second book of devotions as much as we have enjoyed writing them. It is our prayer that your relationship with Christ continues to grow and develop, and that you will live in Him always (Colossians 2:6).

We closed our last book by sharing a prayer for you, and I wanted to do that again. So, as you go from here know that we are continuing to pray for you, and the words Paul wrote to the Colossians would be true of our prayers for you:

We always thank God, the Father of our Lord Jesus Christ, when we pray for you... since the day we heard about you, we have not stopped praying for you and asking God to fill you with the knowledge of his will through all spiritual wisdom and understanding. And we pray this in order that you may live a life worthy of the Lord and may please him in every way: bearing fruit in every good work, growing in the knowledge of God, being strengthened with all power according to his glorious might so that you may have great endurance and patience, and joyfully giving thanks to the Father, who has qualified you to share in the inheritance of the saints in the kingdom of light. For he has rescued us from the dominion of darkness and brought us into the kingdom of the Son he loves, in whom we have redemption, the forgiveness of sins.

~ Colossians 1:3, 9-14

Recommended Resources

Devotions:

Frazzled No More: 30 days to finding Christ's peace for your soul. - www.findyourtruebeauty.com/stress

Teen Devotionals… For Girls! - www.findyourtruebeauty.com/devos

Fuel for the Soul: 21 devotionals that nourish - http://amzn.to/fueldevo

Streams in the Desert - www.crosswalk.com/devotionals/desert

Books:

Mirror, Mirror… Am I Beautiful? – www.truebeautybook.com

Forgiveness Formula - www.theforgivenessformula.com

Bible Reading Plans:

YouVersion - http://www.youversion.com/reading-plans/all

Share Your Thoughts

We would love to hear from you!
To share your thoughts or read what
others had to say, please visit:
www.FindYourTrueBeauty.com

Contact Information:

We would love to hear from you! Send us an e-mail or a letter to the following address:

shelley@shelleyhitz.com
P.O. Box 1757
Findlay, Ohio 45839

Websites:

www.shelleyhitz.com
www.findyourtruebeauty.com
www.truebeautybook.com
www.theforgivenessformula.com

Prayer Requests:

Also, send your prayer requests, so that we can specifically pray for you! You can send them to my address above.

Fixing our eyes on Jesus,

CJ and Shelley Hitz

C.J. and Shelley Hitz enjoy sharing God's Truth through their speaking engagements and their writing. On downtime, they enjoy spending time outdoors running, hiking and exploring God's beautiful creation.

To find out more about their ministry or to invite them to your next event, check out their website at:

www.ChristianSpeakers.tv